The Illustrated Encyclopedia of the

CIVIL WAR

A SALAMANDER BOOK

This edition published in 2001
by Salamander Books
The Chrysalis Building
Bramley Road
London W10 6SP

© 2001 Salamander Books

An imprint of Chrysalis Books Group plc

ISBN 1-84065-307-8

10 9 8 7 6 5 4 3 2

CREDITS
Designed by Phil Clucas and Mark Holt
Featuring the photography of Tria Giovan and Don Eiler

Project Manager: Ray Bonds
Editorial Directors: Will Steeds, Charlotte Davies
Art Director: John Heritage
Production Controller: Peter Colley
Reproduction: Global Colour Separation, Malaysia
Printed and bound in China

The Illustrated Encyclopedia of the
CIVIL WAR

The Soldiers, Generals, Weapons, and Battles

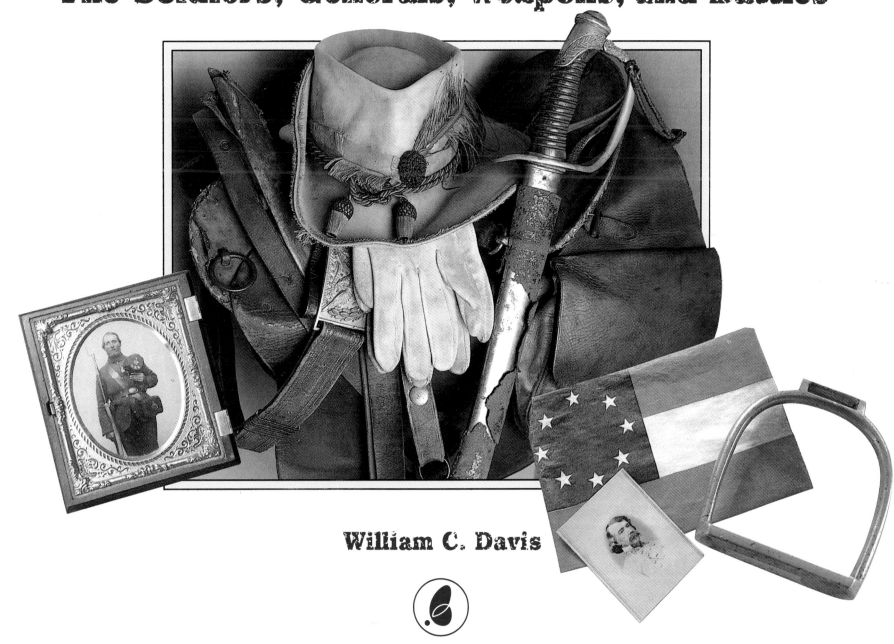

William C. Davis

SALAMANDER

ABOVE: Company M 9th. New York Heavy Artillery

Contents

Introduction 7

INTRODUCTION

Reality so often disappoints expectation. Americans of 1860 lived still mired in the Napoleonic tradition. They expected that warfare should be a pageantry of color and parade, and so they clothed their soldiers in every hue of the rainbow, in uniforms that swept from the drabbest of homespun to *opera buffa* trappings more suited to a hotel hall porter than a fighting man. They believed that men who *looked* and *acted* great would *be* great, and so they gave commands to many men based not on demonstrated ability or military training, but on who gave the best speeches or made the loudest boasts. Like peoples of all times and places, they expected to fight their next war with the tactics of the last one, yet did it cheek-by-jowl with a fascination for the products of a technological explosion of invention and industry that gave them new weapons of unprecedented destructive power. And all of these conceptions, real and false alike, they brought together on their own landscape for four years of the bloodiest conflict ever witnessed in their hemisphere.

These soldiers and generals, the weapons they used and the battlefields they used them on, all made up what for the people of the North and South were the images of the Civil War. All too quickly they learned the shattering difference between their anticipations and the unfolding stark truths of internecine warfare. No one found soldiering to be what was expected. The polish and gaiety of the parade gave way to the endless weeks and months of tedium, stale and rancid food, late pay or no pay at all, life in seas of mud and the parching dust of endless summer. And battle, when it came, and rarely, was not a glorious pageant, but a swirling confusion in which often the lesser of the two mobs called armies was the victor. The generals leading them took years to learn their craft, and some never learned it, paying again and again with the lives of the soldiers for their own ineptitude. The beautiful burnished blades of the sabers and bayonets skewered more meat for the

LEFT: A rare battleflag and Confederate weapons. The top saber is almost homemade, while the other is government issue, as is the kepi. The knife definitely came from home and the pistol was almost a museum piece when the war was fought.

roasting pit than ever they pierced a foe, and first to last Johnny Reb and Billy Yank hurled millions of pounds of raw lead at one another from their devastatingly powerful firearms. Battlefields, in the opening days the objects of picnicking tourists out to see the brilliant battle, became vast killing fields, with once humdrum names like Shiloh Church, Little Round Top, or Wilson's Creek taking on a terrifying shade of meaning.

What the people of the North and South saw then, first in expectation and then in reality, lives again here in the *Illustrated Encyclopedia of the Civil War*. Here is the life of that decidedly *uncommon* common soldier, where he came from, how he trained, what he ate and wore, how he played and prayed, and ultimately how he fought and died. Here, too, are the generals who led him. Some of them were hapless bumblers who brought tragic consequences. Most were workmanlike and competent, many professionals, and a very few, like Lee and Grant, destined to rise above their time and place. In the hands of the men they led were the weapons that decided who died, starting from those left over from an earlier time when the technology for death was not yet so advanced, and ranging through the advent of breech-loading and even repeating rifles, and great cannon capable of sending terrible destruction almost beyond the horizon. And the *Illustrated Encyclopedia of the Civil War* brings all of these elements together on some of the great battlefields of the conflict, from Fort Sumter to Atlanta, from the *Monitor* and the *Virginia* to Petersburg.

Here in a blend of period photographs and artworks and modern views of the artifacts of the war, we can glean the flavor of the people who fought and lived that war, and the kind of life they led. Shed of its romanticism, still the Civil War emerges as a stirring moment in history, replete with deeds that spawn legend and men and women who do seemingly superhuman acts. Their spirit, their wit, their inventiveness, and their willingness to kill and maim in unparalleled numbers, all come through. Most poignant of all are their faces, hundreds of them, the truest and most lasting images of the Civil War. They could almost be *our* faces, and in that not-so-far-off time and place, they were.

THE SOLDIERS

ABOVE: In the end it was the friendships made and the simple, quiet moments that the soldiers remembered and treasured most of all.

THE SOLDIERS

When almost three million men, from North and South, left their homes and went off to war in 1861-1865, despite all the differences that made them fight each other, they had one thing in common. They were embarking upon the greatest experience of their lives. None of them ever had or ever would again live through anything like it. Farmboys who had never left their little villages and counties, and city men to whom the countryside was as foreign as the moon, were all suddenly thrust into a wider world than they had ever known, borne by their feet and their destiny to see America and live life to an extent none of them had dared imagine.

Their paths led them over the dusty, rutted backroads of half a continent, across rivers and streams and through country hamlets destined to achieve immortality thanks to their passing. Wherever the soldiers went they made history, so that more than a century and a quarter later, the greatest moment in the lives of a thousand places on the American map is still the day the armies came. But only when the armies came and stayed for a time did those fields and villages see the other side of Civil War soldiering, the life that the men led every day of the year except for those few that saw them in battle. This other life was the real story of Johnny Reb and Billy Yank.

A sampling of the soldiers' possessions. Carte de visite photos of loved ones, a canteen, a powder flask for a rifle, and a cavalryman's gauntlets, all lie on the most vital bit of all, a home-made blanket, this one belonging to a soldier of the 112th Pennsylvania Infantry.

CHAPTER ONE

GOING TO WAR

ABOVE: Johnny Clem, the "Drummer Boy of Shiloh," shows the youth they all shared.
FACING PAGE: Young men of the Sumter Light Guard at the outset.

There was nothing really sudden about the eruption of war in 1861. When the first guns fired on Fort Sumter on April 12, many had not really expected it, but few were really surprised. North and South had been bickering for two generations, with threats of coming to blows being made almost annually. Thus the young men of America did not have to face a sudden decision when the call to arms went forth after the first shots. They had had years to consider just what they would do, how they would act, on the day that talk turned to blows.

Thousands were already in uniform, members of the uncounted local militia companies, some publicly supported, others privately raised and funded by prominent citizens. Every state had its Home Guard or State Militia as well, and these, too, teemed with fresh-faced boys and enthusiastic, mature men.

Some came for no reason other than the uniform, the chance to parade on Sundays in colorful finery and to carry a big musket with a brightly-polished bayonet. Others answered the tocsin of war out of a spirit of adventure, a sense that this was the chance for a generation to see the country and do great deeds. Most were more serious, however, and in the end ideals of one kind or another put the majority of them into uniforms. The slavery issue accounted

for a number. Genuine antipathy towards the institution existed widely in the North, especially in New England, and many a Yank went off to war with abolition in his heart. Across the lines, a few Southerners went to war chiefly to preserve slavery, though only a few, for not one Confederate in a thousand actually has a personal stake in slavery.

Overwhelmingly, two other causes sent them to war. Northerners enlisted to preserve the Union against separatism, and to avenge the insult to the flag. And the men they were to fight enlisted for no other reason than simply to defend their hearths and Southern homeland from an invader. Those were the primary issues that impelled them to kill each other.

Whatever sent them, from the time they made their decision to go, Reb and Yank alike had much the same experience. They enlisted in small, informal companies in a local village, or went to their county

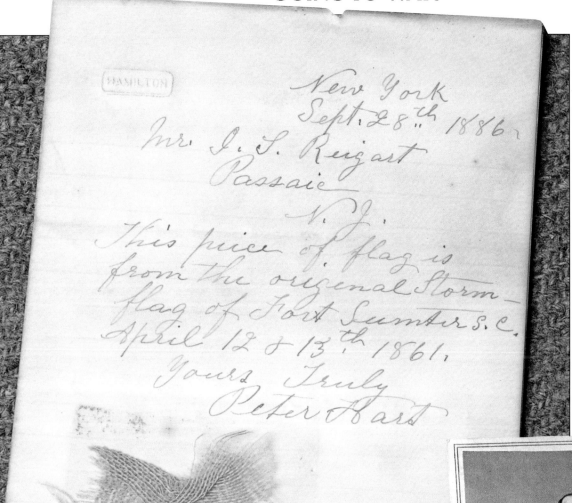

New York
Sept. 28th 1886

Mr. I. S. Reigart
Passaic
N. J.

This piece of flag is
from the original Storm
flag of Fort Sumter S.C.
April 12 & 13th 1861.
Yours Truly
Peter Hart

FACING PAGE TOP: At the firing on Fort Sumter in 1861, all of them, North and South, were new to the business of armies and war. **FACING PAGE BOTTOM:** A typical Union camp scene in the early days of the war. These infantrymen sit before their wall tent, with a rude gutter before it to carry off the rain. Such shelter would be luxury by war's end. **LEFT:** The war produced millions of souvenirs, including this fragment of the storm flag flying over Fort Sumter when it was bombarded, and a letter attesting to its authenticity. **BELOW:** The letter writer was Peter Hart, who fired one of the first answering shots from Sumter.

Serg't Hart.
of Fort Sumter.

THIRD IRISH REGIMENT

25 ABLE-BODIED MEN
CAPTAIN WILLIAMS,
Formerly of the MASS. 24th; now of the 55TH IRISH MASS. REG'T.
Come with us and our IRISH HERO,
CORCORAN
THE GLORY of the other IRISH REGIMENTS,
$150 Bounty
Captain WILLIAMS, or, Lieut. LEONARD!
No. 109 CAMBRIDGE STREET, BOSTON.

TOP: Yankee Militia parade on New York's Broadway in the days before the war. The busby hats would soon disappear.
ABOVE: Recruiting posters like this helped entice and excite hundreds of thousands to enlist.

towns, where the recruiting took on the aspects of a carnival, with marching bands, politicians exhorting their patriotism, and the young ladies waving their scarves and casting swooning eyes on those brave enough to step forward. Indeed, many a boy signed his name or made his mark on the recruiting sergeant's ledger solely because his girlfriend made him. "If a fellow wants to go with a girl now he had better enlist," confessed a pragmatic Indiana lad.

Mostly they were farmers, with a smattering of clerks, tradesmen, mechanics, teachers and the like to fill out their files. Eighty percent of them were under thirty, and some as young as thirteen, and even eleven, managed to slip into the ranks. They did so only because physical examinations consisted

of little more than a thump on the chest and a count to ensure that the proper number of extremities were present. It should come as no surprise, then, that several hundred women managed to enlist and pass examination, posing as men.

These perfunctory formalities concluded, the recruits raised their right hands and swore an oath of allegiance. They were in the army now. Their next step on the road to becoming soldiers was a trip to

FACING PAGE: One of the war's most poignant images is that of Private Edwin Jennison of Georgia, killed in the summer of 1862 when still little more than a boy.
FAR RIGHT: Private Francis E. Brownell of the 11th New York became an overnight Union hero when he killed a Rebel who shot Elmer Ellsworth for taking down a Rebel flag. The flag lies beneath Brownell's foot.

the rendezvous camp, probably nearby, where they got their first taste of rudimentary drill, saw themselves organized more formally into companies and regiments, and perhaps went through the uniquely American volunteer ritual of electing their officers. Soldiers elected their company leaders: lieutenants and a captain, and the company officers then elected the regimental commanders: major, lieutenant colonel, and colonel. If a prominent local

LEFT: Typical field gear for a Yankee sergeant, including belt with bayonet in scabbard, pouch for percussion caps, a shoulder belt, canteen, knapsack and haversack. ABOVE: The typical Confederate could be much less formal, like Georgia's "Racoon Roughs," who lent a colorful cast to Lee's army.

LEFT: The canteen was a vital piece of equipment in both armies. Confederates often carried wooden ones like this, while Yanks' were most often of tin. The awkward forage cap looked ridiculous and very quickly lost favor in the North. Rebs never used them.

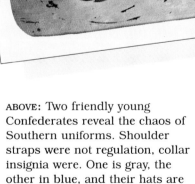

man happened to have funded the uniforms or weapons, or strained himself exceptionally to promote recruiting, he usually got the colonelcy for the asking.

Real training, however, did not come until the recruits were sent off to their camps of instruction, frequently in their state capitals like Camp Curtin in Harrisburg, Pennsylvania, or the host of camps that went up around Richmond, Virginia. However they went, by steamboat, train, or on the soles of their feet, they met a seemingly endless succession of waving crowds and proffered favors along the way. Few of them ever imagined they would kiss as many girls as they did on that brief trip to camp.

The euphoria turned to wearying drudgery all too soon. "The first thing in the morning is drill," a recently arrived recruit wrote home during his first days in instruction camp. "Then drill, then drill again. Then drill, drill, a little more drill. Then drill, and lastly drill. Between drill, we drill and sometimes stop to eat a little and have roll-call." Most of them found it dreadfully confusing, not helped by being dragged out of bed at 5 a.m. or earlier and forced to attempt some evolutions even before their breakfast or the coming of daylight could help awaken their slumbering brains.

Thereafter, and for the rest of the day, their sergeants and officers kept at them constantly, bawling orders and shouting epithets and cursing when confusion inevitably ensued. None of these

ABOVE: Two friendly young Confederates reveal the chaos of Southern uniforms. Shoulder straps were not regulation, collar insignia were. One is gray, the other in blue, and their hats are non-regulation.

ABOVE: A young cavalryman, probably a Confederate, proudly displays his saber and knife, both of them weapons he is likely never to use in battle.

ABOVE RIGHT: Members of New York's famous Irish Brigade show camp informality.

citizen-soldiers would ever become adept parade ground performers. If their leaders could simply get them from point A to point B without their stumbling over each other and getting lost, it was counted as a small victory. It did not help that a number of drill manuals were in use at the time, none agreeing entirely with the others, and when officers and men had been instructed from different books, conflict was inevitable.

The men studied and practiced squad drill, company, battalion, regimental, and even brigade drill, having to learn to recognize commands from voice, drum and bugle. Some manuals called for the memorizing of as many as 64 different trumpet calls. It became even worse when they tried it all while wearing heavy packs and carrying rifles that weighed almost ten pounds. And a soldier with a sharp bayonet at the muzzle of his gun could be a positive menace on the parade ground. More bayonet wounds were inflicted there on some hapless boy in the rank ahead, than in all the combats of the war.

Somehow, though, they got through the weeks of training, much of it perfunctory, especially in the early days when the rush was on to get men to the growing armies. Union General-in-Chief Winfield Scott tried to console one of his commanders in July 1861, before the first battles, saying "you are green, it is true; but they are green, also; you are all green alike." It was certainly true, but slim comfort to the tired, dusty boy who staggered off the parade ground every evening knowing that upon his hurried training, such as it was, might depend his life.

LEFT: The 4th Michigan infantrymen here show the frock coat at right, and the sack coat. Leggings did not last long, and the pistols were not at all regulation for foot soldiers.

ABOVE: Private Charles Pace of Company A, 18th Virginia Infantry, the "Danville Blues," wears one of the Militia uniforms that so many Rebels took to war with them. The shako hat, heavily "frogged" coatee, and white belting, were not at all suited for Civil War campaigning.

CHAPTER TWO

CAMP LIFE

ABOVE: Men of the 22d New York Infantry relax at their drums at Harpers Ferry in 1862.
FACING PAGE: Regulation Union drums from New York, Vermont, and Massachusetts regiments.

Whether at his camp of instruction, or later in the field itself, it was the home away from home that he thus returned to in the evening that he most remembered from his soldiering days. Johnny Reb and Billy Yank both proved terrible soldiers and magnificent fighting men, but they shone best of all when it came to making a life for themselves in their camps.

From the outset they had to leave behind them all their previous notions of what a "home" was like. There were no houses here, no bedrooms, usually not even four walls and a roof. In winter quarters, when the armies remained stationary for three months at a time, the soldiers might build rude log huts with fireplaces and chimneys, and even doors and windows, but for most of the year the common soldier lived and slept in his tent. They came in quite a variety, from the Sibleys, that looked like giant Indian tepees and slept twenty or more in perfect discomfort, down to the lowly "dog tent," made of two halves carried by individual soldiers and buttoned together at night.

Whatever sort of shelter he lived in, the soldier filled it with his few treasured possessions, literally all that he could carry with him in his knapsack or haversack, with perhaps a little extra brought along in the company wagon. Blankets, change of shirt

RIGHT: An 1864 image of winter quarters in Georgia, as General Sherman's "bummers" await the spring campaigning. Scavenged bricks and barrels form chimneys for "houses" made from tents, logs, and whatever else could be found. Many a Southern house found itself stripped to furnish and adorn Yankee huts.

BELOW: Passing the time in camp led to all manner of fun and horseplay, including shamming for the camera. In this case, it was the only swordplay these or any other soldiers were likely to see in the conflict. Their rifles would be their mainstay.

and socks, shaving gear, a Bible, a photograph, and a pitiful few other lowly bits of gear, were all he had.

Most treasured of all, for many, was their mess and cooking kit. It was not much – a frying pan, a coffee boiler perhaps, maybe a few tin plates and cups, with assorted bits of cutlery – but it was highly prized, so much so that in many camps soldiers planned raids on neighboring regiments to steal their cooking ware.

It reflected the fact that the most important single event of the soldier's day was eating. Meals were what broke the tedium of drill or camp policing, the binding experience that brought the men together to relax, either from their labors on the field, or the perpetual boredom of inactivity between campaigns.

Not that what they ate gave them anything to look forward to. In both armies, by any standard, the rations were abominable. The staple of the soldier's diet was euphemistically called "army bread," though it was more generally known as

ABOVE: A lone corporal of the 22d New York poses before his tent at Harpers Ferry in 1862. Its sparse furnishings reveal the meager possessions that a soldier could keep. Even the camp stool was a luxury denied to most. This man probably has all of his vital belongings in the knapsack on his back.

INSET TOP LEFT: A soldier's few simple pleasures might include a candle to cast a feeble light for his pen, a briar pipe onto which he carved the names of his battles, tobacco, and a rude leather kit for sewing or writing materials. INSET LEFT: Mess gear included cutlery, a tin cup, perhaps a covered tin pot for cooking, and whatever was foraged on the way.

MAIN PICTURE: A typical camp scene in Virginia; a Yankee corporal and two sergeants play poker on a homemade table, while a drummer boy looks on. The open door leads into a rude winter hut of logs with a canvas roof. Searching for something to do to fill the endless winter days was a major pastime for men North and South.

FACING PAGE: Among the more photogenic of Union regiments, the 22d New York State Militia displays much of the typical Yankee camp gear. Inside the tent sits a cot, a stack of mess pots and pans, drying laundry, and more. Standard issue blankets air out on neighboring tents, while owners polish their bayonets, read newspapers, or take the sun. **LEFT:** The less glamorous side of winter quarters, when rain and mud turned camps into miserable swamps. The "streets" are corduroyed with branches to escape the mire. **BELOW:** The staple of the soldier's diet was bread, baked in huge batches by thousands of loaves a day. It was issued to soldiers by weight.

hardtack. The soldiers had other names for the three-to-four-inch square, half-inch thick, cracker or biscuit. They came so hard and unchewable that many called them "sheet-iron crackers" and "teeth-dullers." All too often, the hardtack came out of its packing box infested with vermin, leading to its nickname of "maggot hotels" and "worm castles." The soldiers beat them against rocks to knock out most of the inhabitants, then soaked them in water or crushed them under their rifle butts to make them chewable. Flavor was a consideration abandoned early on. To give them any taste at all, the men fried the lumpy, crushed bits in grease to make a hideous fatty mass they called "cush."

Grease was the other staple of their diets. No matter what they ate, it went into the skillet with a

RIGHT: In an era when personal hygiene was at best indifferent, soldiers in the field had little enough to keep themselves tidy. Soap, like the big bar at top right, could be made of lye and burn the skin. Tooth powders and paste were crude and abrasive. Toothbrushes lost their bristles easily, and straight razors lost their edge. Many men opted for beards instead. Combs were made from ivory, bone, or gutta-percha. The white cotton or linen towels were a genuine rarity, and all such sanitary items proved scarce after 1861; in the South they became almost collectors' items.

RIGHT: In the endless pursuit of entertainment, sports were a popular diversion, including the relatively young game of baseball. The walnut bat was used during the war, as was the leather ball. The red fireman's shirt is typical of the clothing worn by players, and the silver shield pin at upper right shows crossed bats. The photo is of George Muzzey, who played regularly at events like that in the handbill.

helping of lard or fat. Fresh vegetables were often in short supply, or else came in a dehydrated block of shreds that expanded prodigiously when placed in water. The men called them "desiccated" vegetables. Even worse was the meat ration. Only rarely was it fresh. More often it came as "pickled" beef or pork, preserved in a smelly brine, or else dried and heavily salted. "Bully beef," they called it, or "salt horse," or even "blue beef," thanks to its occasional color when the pickling failed to hold off the onset of putrefaction. Sometimes it arrived so glutinous from decomposition that the men joked about throwing it against trees to watch it stick and quiver. More than one company mess took a particularly evil meat ration and gave it a mock burial instead of eating it. No wonder that no farmer's field or livestock pen was safe when the armies were about. No wonder, too, that so many

TOP LEFT: An assortment of camp goods includes a coffee boiler, ladles and sieves, mess plates, a salt or sugar shaker, a combination knife-fork-spoon, tin cups, and a coffee bean roaster.

TOP RIGHT: To keep them dry, soldiers kept matches, or "locofocos," in metal match "safes" like the one at bottom. The straight razor is far more ornate than most, while the pocket corkscrew and pick shows much use.

LEFT: Officers and non-com's had more ornate finery, from epaulettes to belt sashes, and perhaps an album for carte de visites of members of the regiment.

men suffered almost continually from stomach and bowel disorders, thanks to the ponds of grease in which they cooked this rank mess to give it some flavor, or to hide the flavor it already had.

The best times came in the evenings, when all the drill was done. In summer, and on fall days especially, when the light lasted late, they sat around their tents or their fires and entertained themselves as have soldiers of all times. They wrote prodigiously, literally millions of letters and tens of thousands of diaries. Even the illiterate could pass the time by dictating a letter home to a more lettered comrade. Those who could read did so, devouring whatever they could find: newspapers, cheap novels, the Bible, political tracts, and sometimes even camp newspapers prepared and printed by fellow soldiers.

Almost every mess had at least one boy who could strum a guitar or banjo, or play a fiddle. Music echoed about the camps every night, and if most of it was not very good, still it lifted the hearts of the listeners. A few regiments even fielded small bands to entertain, often augmented by groups of amateur

FACING PAGE: Quiet moments in camp found those who could read studying letters from home, like the two at left, or writing in a diary, or just looking on and enjoying the interlude.
ABOVE: By contrast, men wanting more energetic entertainment staged theatricals and "stag" dances, with competition often keen.
LEFT: Every regiment had a few musicians, or even a band, to provide music for campfire and other entertainments. Some outfits even had glee clubs and debating societies.

INSET TOP LEFT: Smoking became one of the soldiers' chief pleasures, and tobacco a major commodity of trade between the armies. Cigars and pipes abounded, as did the ubiquitous match safes. INSET BOTTOM LEFT: Nothing suited a good smoke like a game of chance. Soldiers gambled incessantly at dice, cards - some printed with martial scenes - even chess. INSET BOTTOM RIGHT: The lowly coffee grinder gave them their favorite drink. MAIN PICTURE: Tobacco, cards, and beer or wine, made the ideal afternoon.

ABOVE: Women in the camps were not an uncommon sight. Many were wives of officers who joined their husbands during winter quarters or in garrison, like this lady with an Illinois battery at Chattanooga. During active campaigning, however, they stayed in the rear or went back home. Some with the armies acted as laundresses.

actors and glee clubs. One Kentucky Confederate brigade even had its own debating society. Hundreds of songs enjoyed popularity North and South, but one outshone them all, signifying the longing of the boys to return to their "Home, Sweet Home."

The rest of the time they took their fun where they could find it. In winter, a fresh snowfall was sure to produce snowball battles, some of epic proportions, like the one in the Army of Tennessee in March 1864, when whole divisions battled each other, taking prisoners and inflicting not a few wounds, all in the name of fun. They put on races and bet their meager pay on anything that would move, from cockroaches dropped onto heated plates, to men riding razorback hogs, or others pushing

comrades seated in wheelbarrows. They played baseball – already an old game by the time of the war – used cannon balls for bowling at ten-pins, and even dabbled in a rude variant of cricket. They whittled sticks, carved pipes from soapstone, mended their garments, stared at the evening skies and daydreamed, and most of all just sat around the coffee boiler and talked, fighting their old battles over and over again, and boasting of what they would do when they got their next crack at Reb or Yank.

Above everything else, they made friends, the kind of friendships that lasted for lifetimes, as they spent their youth and risked their lives on the battlefields of North and South.

LEFT: Some winter quarters were virtual cities, with populations of tens of thousands and cabins laid out in blocks along streets that were given names. This hut city in Virginia might have a library, a theater, and even a concert hall, all built of logs and canvas, and all destined to be abandoned with the coming of spring. Whole forests disappeared in the wake of the passing armies.

RIGHT: Winter huts being built at Fort Brady, Virginia in 1864 by the 1st Connecticut Heavy Artillery. The location on a downslope may come to be a curse when rain runs down the hillside, and into the huts. Still, it made homes, of a sort.

CHAPTER THREE

THE SOMBER SIDE

ABOVE: One of Illinois' monuments to her sons. **FACING PAGE INSET LEFT:** Americans would dot the landscape with memorials and (inset right) cemeteries. **OPPOSITE:** Rebel dead.

ew of these bright-faced young men anticipated the horrors that awaited them away from the battle-field, and fewer still ever suspected that their own camp habits more often than not exposed them to those dangers. Thanks to his hideous diet and inadequate camp sanitation, almost every soldier reported for sick call more than once during the war. Medicines were few and of little value, and some were actually dangerous, being based largely on opiates, arsenic, and lead. The cures were all too often more severe than the ills.

But worse still were the epidemics that swept through the armies. Never before had so many men congregated in so confined an area. Tens of thousands of rural boys had grown up without ever being exposed to ordinary childhood diseases. As a result, measles, mumps, chicken pox, scarlet fever, and more, killed thousands in the early months of the war. Typhoid and diphtheria, thanks to contaminated water, swept through whole regiments. By the end of the war, Yankee surgeons – the only ones who kept adequate records – determined that more than six million cases of illness had been treated, and those were just the ones that were reported. With something over a quarter million soldiers wearing the blue in the conflict, that meant that every soldier, on average,

went before a physician at least twice, and some repeatedly. They complained of loose bowels, scurvy, smallpox, pneumonia, rheumatism, and more. Typhoid killed at least 100,000, while dysentery accounted for even more of the 400,000 or more in blue and gray who died from germs rather than bullets.

But bullets, too, accounted for their share, and woe to the man struck by one of those gigantic missiles. When a lump of lead, varying from half to three-quarters of an inch thick and an inch long, slammed into a man's body it inflicted terrible damage. Often as not, the man was killed almost instantly, especially if struck in the head, neck, or upper torso. Otherwise, if the slug severed enough veins or arteries on its cruel path, a soldier could bleed to death before receiving aid, and even in spite of it given the crude means available for staunching bleeding. Surviving even that, he could die of simple shock.

FACING PAGE: Some of thousands of Confederate dead at Gettysburg in 1863. Burial details worked for weeks, and coffins had to be reserved for Union casualties.
ABOVE: Only the crudest of markers could be made for Rebel dead like these, most of whom would lie unidentified and lost.
LEFT: Other war dead lay in neat rows in places like Andersonville, Georgia, the prison camp that claimed the lives of thousands of captured Federals.

SURGICAL STAFF.

Some argued that those who died outright were the lucky ones. For the rest, any torso or head wound was regarded as virtually untreatable. They were given whatever pain-killer was available, if available, and made as comfortable as possible. That was all. If they survived and healed, it was on their own, for military medicine could do nothing for them. More often than not, infection killed them if they survived everything else.

LEFT AND FACING PAGE: The green sash of a U.S. Army Surgeon, with his sword belt and shoulder straps of a lieutenant-colonel, showing the insignia of the Medical Corps. INSET: A Surgical Staff arm band.

Arm and leg wounds were "treatable," however, and got priority at the field hospitals. A lucky man had a bullet pass through the fleshy part of an extremity, missing the bone altogether. With the entry and exit wounds stitched shut, he had a chance of relatively full recovery if gangrene did not set in. But when the projectile hit a bone, it shattered it, and almost the only known treatment was

ABOVE: Some of the apparatus most feared by soldiers – the bandages, and other implements used when men are wounded. Some were fortunate to have even these crude aids.

amputation. Indeed, even in flesh wounds where healing refused to take place, removing the limb was standard procedure.

In any such operation, there was no concept at all of asepsis or sterilization. Surgeons worked with filthy hands and instruments, passing millions of germs and infection from one patient to the next, and leading soldiers to agree with one boy who claimed that "hell will be Filde with do[c]tors … when this war is over." Contrary to later popular myth, almost all amputations and other operations, even in the Confederacy, were performed under some form of general anaesthetic, usually laudanum. But this only postponed the pain, for recovery from amputations was long and traumatic, and treatable only with more laudanum or opiates. In many cases the pain and treatments lasted for years, and the decade after the Civil War saw more drug addiction in America than at any time until the post-World War II generations turned to it for recreation.

ABOVE: Union field ambulance men at practice removing wounded. In battle men often lay for hours waiting for attention. **RIGHT:** A field hospital and surgery at Gettysburg, with an amputation – probably staged – taking place. **FACING PAGE TOP:** Nurse Ann Bell tending Union wounded. **BOTTOM LEFT:** Yankee wounded in a field hospital in 1863. **CENTER:** A wounded boy not yet old enough to legally enlist. **BOTTOM RIGHT:** A home in South Carolina turned into a hospital for Union wounded. Hundreds of homes and warehouses had their floors stained with blood by the wounded of both sides.

Even the soldier whose health and constitution resisted the dangers lurking in his camp, and whose luck on the battlefield kept him from the bullets' path, could still face these same nightmares if it became his misfortune to be captured by the enemy. During the war some 425,000 men in blue and gray – 15 percent of those who served – fell into enemy hands and were sent to prison camps

BELOW: Medicines of the era were crude at best, and a surgeon's pharmacy like this might consist chiefly of sulphur and opium and mercury compounds, many capable of more harm than good. Time did most of the healing.

scattered all across the continent. Contrary to post-war charges of cruelty and barbarism, there was little wilful mistreatment of prisoners on either side. The men suffered for the same reasons that they suffered in their own camps: bad hygiene, terrible nutrition, and exposure to the elements and the myriad germs that flourished in the rich human soup formed when up to 30,000 at a time were confined in the space of barely more than twenty acres.

In fact, most prisons soon became glorified hospitals. Andersonville boasted 33,000 inhabitants at one point, making it the fifth largest "city" in the Confederacy, and half its population was perpetually

FACING PAGE FAR LEFT: Like medieval instruments of torture, the surgeons' knives and saws struck terror in men's hearts. **ABOVE LEFT:** Hospital stewards enjoying a drink. Many a medico sought too much solace in alcohol. **BELOW LEFT:** A Yankee field hospital after battle shows the results of bullets and surgeons' handiwork.

FACING PAGE TOP: A dread even greater than of injury or death for many soldiers was the thought of being captured by the enemy. Prison camps North and South were nightmares, as these Confederates captured in 1864 are about to learn. Many will not survive. FACING PAGE BOTTOM: Among the most notorious hell-holes was Richmond's Libby Prison, where Yankee officers were kept. THIS PAGE FAR RIGHT: What a man could look like in time.

on the sick list. Northern compounds like Fort Delaware were only marginally better. Prisoners in the Confederacy suffered a harder lot only because everyone in the South was worse off than their Yankee counterparts. Rebel jailors fed and clothed their captives to almost the same standard as their own soldiers in the field, and in some of the more remote areas west of the Mississippi prisoners may

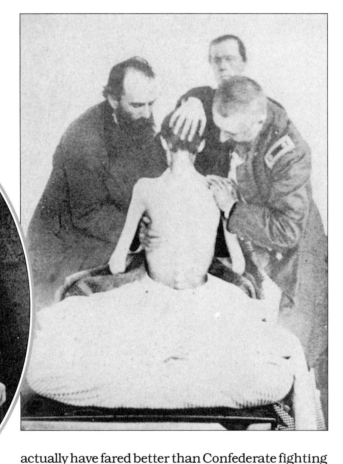

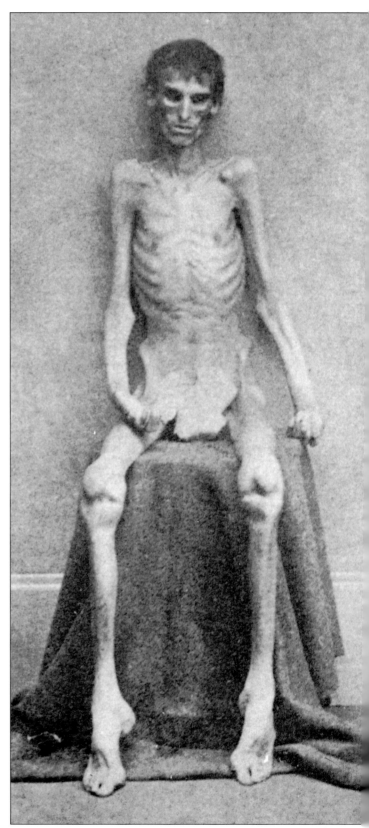

ABOVE: This poor Yank shows in his body the hardship of confinement at Andersonville in Georgia. ABOVE CENTER: Another Andersonville survivor being examined by army doctors, and apparently too weak to sit up unassisted.

actually have fared better than Confederate fighting men. In the Union, prisoners received generally much better fare, with more regular issues of clothing, blankets, and other necessities. Still, nutrition was poor, and the commissary general for prisoners of war, William Hoffman, rationalized that men leading a sedentary existence as captives needed less nourishment than active soldiers, and reduced their ration in 1863. It was not, again, intentional cruelty, but merely the ignorance of dietary needs shared by all men of the time, but Hoffman's action undoubtedly worsened the lot of thousands in his care.

Despite their hardships, the men in the prison compounds coped somehow, finding even humor and camaraderie in their misery. They told tall tales of the regiments of lice and bedbugs that shared their quarters, turned their gallows humor to betting on the number of dead at the end of each day, even made games of trapping mice and rats for extra food. To relieve the endless hours of boredom, they wrote and read, sang, and engaged in the perpetual idle speculation about release or exchange, most of which rumors proved to be cruelly unfounded. A very few put their minds to devising means of escape, either by tunneling, sneaking away from a work or wood-gathering detail outside the compound, or even hiding among the dead taken outside for burial. In the end, though a number of spectacular breakouts occurred, no more than one or two in a thousand ever successfully got away. The rest just sat, and waited, and endured.

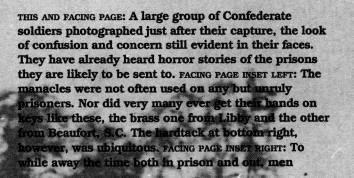

THIS AND FACING PAGE: A large group of Confederate soldiers photographed just after their capture, the look of confusion and concern still evident in their faces. They have already heard horror stories of the prisons they are likely to be sent to. FACING PAGE INSET LEFT: The manacles were not often used on any but unruly prisoners. Nor did very many ever get their hands on keys like these, the brass one from Libby and the other from Beaufort, S.C. The hardtack at bottom right, however, was ubiquitous. FACING PAGE INSET RIGHT: To while away the time both in prison and out, men fashioned trinkets like these identity badges from bits of bone. THIS PAGE INSET BOTTOM LEFT: Prisoners were thrown on their own initiative to pass the time or entertain themselves. This watercolor by a Rebel at the Point Lookout, M.D., camp illustrates a minstrel show put on by his fellow prisoners. THIS PAGE INSET BOTTOM RIGHT: More than anything else, the prisoner worried about his stomach and keeping it filled. Rations were indifferent even at the best compounds, with starvation a possibility. The lowly hardtack, moldy, worm-infested, brittle, was still the soldier's friend.

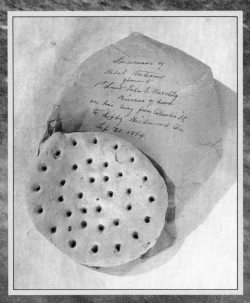

CHAPTER FOUR

BETWEEN HEAVEN AND HELL

What sustained many a captive was the almost universal religion that pervaded the armies. Johnny Reb and Billy Yank came from a religious time and place, when the church played a major role not just spiritually but in society as well. Almost every regiment went to war with a chaplain, usually protestant except in predominantly Irish or European outfits where Catholics were most numerous. Even a few rabbis went to war, though soldiers often subordinated their individual denominations in order to attend whatever services were available. They met in the afternoons or evenings on Sundays, and when no chaplain was available an officer gave the sermon, or even one of the men in the ranks. In the Army of Northern Virginia, General William N. Pendleton, chief of artillery, often reverted to his pre-war occupation by giving sermons, and in the Army of Tennessee several Rebel generals held forth from the pulpit. Stonewall Jackson himself sometimes spoke, but more often passed through the ranks handing out religious tracts.

Religious revivals twice swept through the Confederate forces, probably in response to the sense of desperation for their cause and the need for divine intervention. Most notable was the one that hit the Army of Tennessee in the winter of 1863-64, when services were held nightly

ABOVE: Chaplains like Thomas Scully fought for men's souls.
FACING PAGE: A pastor in battle.

BELOW: The wares of many a chaplain – glasses, crucifix, amulet, and a container for the holy Host. **BOTTOM RIGHT:** The United States Sanitary Commission passed out cups for soldiers' personal needs, and Bibles for their spirits.

throughout the army, with everyone from generals down to lowly privates participating. At least some of the impetus came from boredom; attending frequent services helped to pass the time, and some soldiers even took to rating the several chaplains according to their speaking merits. But mostly the interest came from genuine concern, and thousands were baptized in the fervor.

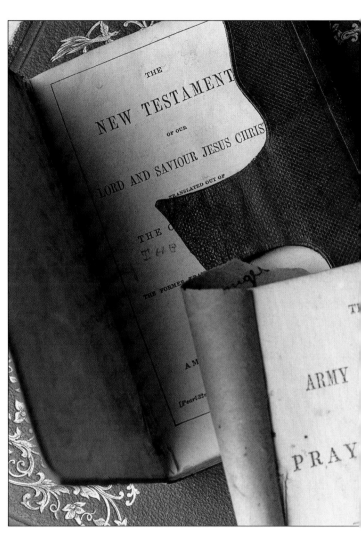

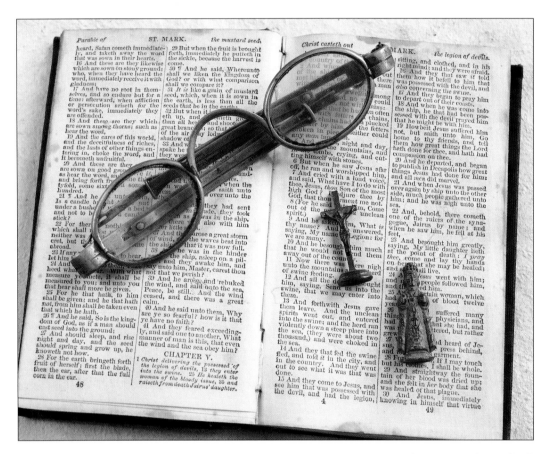

THIS AND FACING PAGE CENTER: The Sanitary and the United States Christian Commission distributed thousands of New Testaments and prayer books like these, though these are, in fact, Confederate publications sold or distributed by "relief" societies. **FACING PAGE FAR RIGHT:** A Yankee chaplain at his rude pulpit.

Special organizations North and South worked to further the ends of religion in the camps. The United States Christian Commission sent its agents throughout the Union armies, passing out Bibles, tracts and song sheets, providing wholesome reading matter of other kinds, conducting services in camps, and providing spiritual counseling to men who felt the need. The U.S. Sanitary Commission also did much the same work, though chiefly concentrating its efforts on day-to-day comforts for the men. In the South, a number of similar organizations did what they could, mostly on a state basis, like the Kentucky Relief Society.

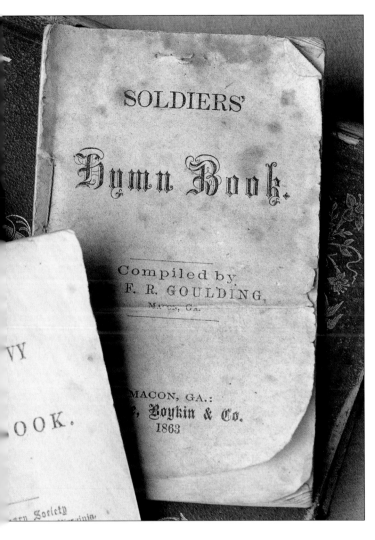

They had their work cut out for them, for maintaining the spiritual and physical morale of the Civil War soldier was a full-time job, and temptations lay at every turn. Most of these men had never been outside their home counties before, but now they were in the great, wide world, and in the company of tens of thousands of earthy, often rebellious, and very red-blooded fellow males.

Profanity was the least of their sins, and it prevailed at every level. Generals like Jubal Early and Joseph Hooker were reputed to "swear" their men into battle, while the lowly private soldiers brought with them from their homes every conceivable variety of oath, some wondrous for their inventiveness. While universally condemned, still it was a useful release for tension and frustration, and few soldiers ever suffered punishment for foul

BELOW: Chaplain Thomas Tipton's stern stare may betray the considerable battle that he and fellow ministers fought in trying to save men's souls from the degrading influences of army life.

RIGHT: The chaplain of New York's famous "Fighting 69th" holds a Sunday Mass for men of the predominantly Catholic regiment. Colonel Michael Corcoran stands just left with arms folded, with other officers on either side of the improvised tent-chapel.

language, unless they unwisely directed it to an officer's face. Behind their backs, officers were almost universal objects of some of the more ingenious epithets.

A soldier stepped onto more dangerous ground when he took a drink – or several. There was no official liquor ration in either army, though some regiments did occasionally dole out a tot to the men. But Reb and Yank alike showed remarkable resourcefulness in finding it on their own. Most of what they drank was of miserable quality, called "mean" whiskey as a rule, but often dubbed with more colorful nicknames like "Rock Me to Sleep, Mother," "Who Hit John," or "Bust-head" and "Rot of Pop-Skull."

The names said it all, and when a soldier took too much he was apt to perform all manners of infractions, from insubordination or insolence to an officer, to brawling, desertion, or worse. Some commanders believed that virtually all the ills

BELOW: The source of most misbehavior by soldiers was the bottle – or any of several bottles like these beer, wine, and spirits containers. The drink was often crudely made, and quite justifiably given a variety of epithets by the men who consumed it.

besetting discipline in the armies stemmed from drunkenness, and some took draconian measures to curb the vice. Medical stores of brandy and whiskey had to be kept under lock and guard. Towns under occupation sometimes saw their supplies of liquor confiscated, and in Richmond President Jefferson Davis threatened to banish alcohol from the city entirely if the merchants and officers could not control its access to the men in the ranks.

RIGHT AND FACING PAGE: Sometimes soldier misbehavior called for the ultimate penalty. Though this shows the execution of Andersonville Commandant Henry Wirz, any maximum sentence would look the same.

An inevitable concomitant to the rough comradeship of the bottle was gambling, and games of every sort were played in the camps, from endless varieties of poker, to "chuck-a-luck," keno, euchre, and more. Dice rolled across blankets turned into informal crap tables, and the men bet on everything imaginable, including cockfights. The officers tried continually to curtail gambling, but to no avail.

ABOVE: The offending soldier's fate lay in the hands of the court-martial, like this one sitting in New Hampshire in 1863. Sentences could vary from the humiliating and uncomfortable, like being bound to a wagon wheel (right), to having to carry a ball and chain (facing page top left), or wearing a wooden barrel (facing page top right), or even being drummed out of the army with head shaved (facing page bottom), and sometimes branded according to the offense.

The story was the same with the illicit delights of the flesh. Camp followers and prostitutes appeared wherever the armies went, and in some of the major cities, especially Washington and Richmond, they openly flourished. For many a boy released from the inhibiting restraints of his home and community, such feminine temptations were too much to resist. As a result, rights over women provided further breaches of discipline, while venereal disease was rampant in some regiments.

For all of these offenses and more, the authorities meted out a variety of penalties, more in the nature of punishment for its own sake than out of any real hope that such treatments might actually act as inhibiting factors on the men's behavior. All punishments were humiliating, and most were painful as well. A spell in the guard house, confinement to quarters, rations of nothing but bread and water, were commonly used for minor infractions. A man could also be made to walk the

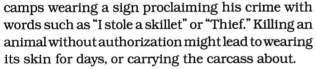

camps wearing a sign proclaiming his crime with words such as "I stole a skillet" or "Thief." Killing an animal without authorization might lead to wearing its skin for days, or carrying the carcass about.

More serious offenses resulted in wearing a ball and chain affixed to the ankle, or carrying a heavy log about camp for hours. Worse yet was riding a wooden "horse" or fence rail, and worse even than that was being tied spread-eagled to a wagon wheel for several hours, or being "bucked and gagged" – hands and ankles bound, seated on the ground with knees drawn up and a stick run under them and over the inside of the elbow. A man could be tied up by his thumbs, and in some cases even flogged. Cowardice in action could bring branding with a "C" on the forehead, and the worst crimes – murder, treason, desertion, rape – brought death by hanging or firing squad. It was not an era in which the wise man stepped too far over the line, for punishment could be swift and severe.

CHAPTER FIVE

THE TEST OF BATTLE

ABOVE: A rather fanciful depiction of Federal soldiers clambering up Lookout Mountain, near Chattanooga, Tennessee during the famous "Battle Above the Clouds."

Red-blooded as they were, Yank and Reb alike, the soldiers in the ranks were, in the overwhelming majority, relatively law-abiding men when donned their uniforms to fight, not to make mischief. And when they fought, they could be magnificent. Throughout the history of warfare, the battle has been the ultimate moment of soldiering, the goal toward which all the rest – the training, the building of camaraderie and loyalty, even the fun and mischief – is directed. It was in the face of battle that these men found themselves, and showed the world who they were.

It was an almost indescribable time during the hours and then final moments leading up to firing the first shot and feeling the first heat of combat. "The feeling called *fear* did not enter my breast," a Tennessee Rebel wrote just after his first fight in May 1862, "but it was painful, nervous anxiety, a longing for action … and a dull feeling about the chest that made breathing difficult." Another Confederate, writing fitfully in his diary while marching toward the sound of the guns at Shiloh in April 1862, felt much the same. "I have the shakes badly," he confessed. "Oh how I wish I was a dwarf, just now, instead of a six-footer."

Indeed, whatever their fears in the weeks leading up to their first combat, almost all men found in the

LEFT: A typical Union infantryman of the war, the man upon whose bravery in battle the hopes of the Union depended so heavily. He is armed with a Harpers Ferry rifled musket and triangular bayonet, wears a belt that holds his cartridge box on his left hip with a smaller box for percussion caps in front, and his bayonet scabbard on his right hip. His courage and his rifle will be the workhorses of the war. BELOW: Some soldiers were issued powder flasks like this one. The funnel on top measured the proper charge for a rifle load, though soldiers universally preferred paper-wrapped "cartridges" instead.

ABOVE: Many thousands of Yankees sat out much of the war in garrisons behind the line, or, like these men of a heavy artillery unit, serving in one of the dozens of forts ringing Washington and other cities deemed vulnerable to Confederate attack. Except during a July 1864 raid by Jubal Early's corps, these soldiers and their rifles and cannon may have gone through the war without firing a shot. FACING PAGE BOTTOM: A Yankee artillery battery of Parrott rifles in formation for battle in Virginia. Ammunition carriages stand behind the guns and further caissons at the rear.

end that, instead of terror at the last moment, they felt a crushing anxiety to get into the fight, a hurry to get it started and done with, perhaps because it meant that all the long waiting would finally be over.

"With your first shot you become a new man," said a Confederate who himself became a "new man" at the First Battle of Bull Run. "Fear has no existence in your bosom. Hesitation gives way to an uncontrollable desire to rush into the thickest of the fight." A first-timer on the other side of the line found the same thing. "After the first round the fear left me," wrote this Billy Yank, "and I was as cool as ever I was in my life."

That first shot was an experience that bound them all to a fraternity stronger than all the issues that divided them. Early on the morning of battle the drums and bugles awakened them – assuming they had been able to sleep, that is, for no battle came as a surprise, and most men, veterans and neophytes alike, spent fitful evenings before a battle,

many writing what they feared to be their last letters home, or putting their names and addresses on slips of paper tucked into their pockets so that, if killed, they could be identified and their bodies sent home. Once awakened, the soldier ate a hurried breakfast if there was time, or more likely gulped some coffee and crunched on a hardtack while rushing to his place in the column.

By dawn, the cannon fire and skirmishers' peppering away could probably be heard a few miles ahead. The men fell in line. "I can never forget my thoughts as I stood there and looked around," wrote a Tennessean in 1862. He looked around at his comrades, some boys he had known since youth, and realized for the first time that in a few hours time some of them might be dead. He watched as they made sorry attempts to jest and be jaunty, knowing that they felt the same fear as he did. Curiously, right in those moments, the fear that men felt was not of pain and death, but that they would turn coward and run in front of their braver

fellows. "I am afraid that the groans of the wounded & dying will make me shake," confessed one Federal, while a Rebel boy admitted after his first fight that "though i did not run i mite have run if i had thought of it in time."

Rapidly the men marched to the sound of the guns. Then they were halted somewhere behind the battle line while their officers got their orders. These were the worst moments of all. Mouths dry, palms sweaty, they clung to the ground, checked to make certain their bayonets were fixed and their rifles ready, and disappeared into their thoughts. In those last minutes, though the battlefield might teem with 200,000 men, every soldier was dreadfully, painfully alone.

If his generals were standing on the defensive, holding a good piece of ground, the soldier's first sight of the battlefield might have been from behind a farmer's rail or stone fence, a hastily dug rifle pit, or log and earth breastworks. Once there, he had more waiting in store. First the enemy's artillery would open up on his position, trying to blast his defenses with solid shot, or disrupt the formations manning it with exploding shells. Sitting out the barrage, the man knew that it was only the prelude

BELOW: A black fighting man of the famous 54th Massachusetts Infantry, one of the fortunate survivors of the bloody July 1863 assault on Fort Wagner, South Carolina. He and others settled the question of whether the black would fight.

FACING PAGE: The soldiers told the stories of their battles, their bravery and their fears, most effectively in their letters home. Millions were written North and South. LEFT: Company I of the 6th Pennsylvania cavalry was better known as the "Rush Lancers," one of a few early war units equipped with outdated lances they never used. BELOW: A cavalry charge in the battle of Gaines' Mill in June 1862. It is more than fanciful, for the mounted charge was even then on its way to being a thing of the past.

to the enemy's charge. In a few minutes – though sometimes not until after an hour of shelling – the cannon fell silent and the foe appeared, rank by rank, in the distance, bayonets gleaming, flags fluttering, and all sporadically seen through the pall of gunsmoke that hung low and sluggish over the field. Bugles and shouts announced the charge, and then the sight of them running toward him, throats lustily giving forth their battle cries, while his own artillery behind him opened up with case-shot and canister, trying to break up the charge before it reached the works. Seeing several thousand screaming men rushing toward him, a soldier could feel very solitary indeed.

If he were on the other side, however, the story was different, and in a way easier. At least there he was not sitting through the shelling, not looking over the field to see the masses arrayed against him. He felt a part of the mass as his regiment, brigade, division, or even corps, marshalled its ranks for the charge. Fear was forgotten in the rush to get everything ready. There was no time in these last moments for anything but remembering what he was supposed to do. Then came the bugles and

drums, the swaggering officers, the anxious hush along the line, and the order to go.

Contrary to popular mythology, very few combats ever came down to hand-to-hand fighting, and bayonets inflicted so few wounds on an enemy as to be virtually worthless. An indefinable moment came in an attack when one side or the other flinched first. Most assaults failed, thanks to the power that rifled weapons gave to well-placed defenders, and the shock value of thundering artillery backing up the defenders. When an attack succeeded, it generally did so – as at Missionary Ridge in November 1863 – by the defenders being psychologically beaten by the sight of what was coming towards them, and abandoning their position before the enemy actually arrived. In time the men learned this. They also learned to keep their eyes straight ahead, to worry about seemingly mundane things like the rocks on the ground before them, not stumbling, and keeping close to the rest of the men in their lines.

FACING PAGE: Battle as boys fancied it before going to war. The reality proved to be a rude awakening when it came – all confusion, smoke and noise, with little of the glorious.

Of course, no man could shut his eyes to the horrors taking place around him. "I have Seen," one Yankee wrote home, "men rolling in their own blood." "They lay mangled and torn to pieces so that Even friends could not tell them." A Georgia boy confessed the "you doant know what kind of a-feeling it put on me to see men shot down like hoges & See a man tore all to peases with a Shell after he is dead." And for those who were really active in the slaughter, the effect could be even more traumatic. "I shot men," confessed a Mississippian, "until my heart was sick at the slaughter."

ABOVE: For more than half a million, this is what the war came to, death in a muddy Petersburg trench, a hospital, or a prison camp. TOP: The "fortunate" ones at least went to their final rest with their names. Thousands would be listed simply as "unknown" to posterity.

ABOVE: A typical Yankee outfit, Company C of the 110th Pennsylvania Infantry, shows the youthful, sometimes shambling, sometimes erect, face that Rebs and Yanks alike turned to their foe in some 10,000 engagements large and small. Some were heroes, some were cowards, most were simply patriots caught up in the greatest event of their time.

Then it was over. Such scenes might be repeated a dozen times in a day, for two or three days running in a major battle, but at last came the moment when one side or the other quit the field, or both armies simply sat down and stared at each other, too weary to fight on. The physical and emotional let-down was profound. "I did not know how tired I was until the excitement of the battle was over," wrote a Minnesota boy after the Battle of Gaines' Mill in June 1862. "I was almost too weak to stand, and my cheeks as hollow as though emaciated by a long spell of sickness." He collapsed under a bush "and slept such a sleep as comes only to a tired soldier after a battle."

Heroism was a relative term in the Civil War. Few distinguished themselves above their fellows for heroism, and yet any man who could stand up to the horrors of the battlefield, and the terrors in his own heart, was a hero of sorts if he did not turn and flee. In fact, of course, there were heroes a-plenty, caused as much by circumstance, luck and accident as by any conscious design. In the Union, the War Department in 1862 established the Medal of Honor. It was awarded both to honor those who stretched themselves beyond what was normally expected of a soldier in the face of the enemy, as well as to provide an incentive to others, a source of pride to men and regiments and families back

home. Jefferson Davis, too, authorized a Confederate Medal of Honor, but it was never issued, and instead men who distinguished themselves had their names added to a "Roll of Honor" that was read aloud to the armies after battles and published in the press. One actual medal was awarded, to a tiny band of defenders of the fort at Sabine Pass, Texas, when a silver dollar was milled flat and inscribed with the name of the action.

The war taught the soldiers blue and gray a valuable lesson in an era not noted for its tolerance. Heroism came in all colors and nationalities. Irish, German, Polish, Protestant, Catholic, Jew, white, black, or red, men in battle behaved the same. Several thousand American Indians served in each army, and many distinguished themselves, adding heroism to other notable attributes like names such as Jumper Duck, George Hogtotoer, Big Mush Dirt Eater, and more. Mexican-Americans, too, served in the armies, especially in the Confederate service under officers like Refugio Benavides. And some 180,000 free blacks and former slaves donned the Union blue. Most never saw real action, but when they did, as with the spectacular, doomed attack of the 54th Massachusetts on Battery Wagner in July 1863, they proved that, whether skin was white or black, blood was only red, and valor knew no color.

ABOVE: One thing that experience at war did not change was the devotion of soldiers to their regimental banners; men literally died protecting their colors, or proudly vied for the opportunity to carry them aloft in the forefront of battle, as in this Union charge during the Battle of Cold Harbor, Virginia on June 1, 1864. The color-bearer's was the shortest life expectancy in the outfit. LEFT: Rebel cavalry carry the Confederate "battleflag" with the same reverence that they devoted to it for generations after the war.

THE UNIFORMS

ABOVE: Men believed to be with the 12th New York Regiment in 1861 in uniforms typifying the early war variety. Some wear frock coats, others shell jackets. Some have forage caps, others slough hats, or headgear brought from home. One (seated, left) wears a zouave-type outfit.

CHAPTER SIX

THE CONFEDERATE SOLDIER

ABOVE: A Confederate infantryman in crudely manufactured "butternut" frock coat and with bayonet-mounted musket. He is actually one of three brothers who joined the same regiment.

When armed conflict began, lack of uniformity in dress of troops was a major problem. Many Rebel units didn't have gray, so they fought in what they often termed "butternut" uniforms. Close to the end of the war, North Carolina textile mills turned out a big batch of Confederate uniforms before taking care that they had suitable dyes on hand. When no gray could be found, these were dyed blue – and shipped off for use by Confederate units. This inevitably led to numerous instances in which comrades fired upon comrades.

What the Rebel soldier wore showed the deplorable state of Confederate supply. Scores of regiments equipped themselves locally before going off to war, but as clothing and equipment wore out it was often up to the private soldier to replace it himself. Even what the Richmond government did manage to distribute was often of wildly varying quality. Uniforms alone varied from gray so dark as to be almost blue, to "butternuts" and browns – all of it supposedly the official "cadet gray." As for the items prescribed as "regulation issue," only a few regiments raised early in the war ever got them all. In time, an issue of new socks would be a memorable day.

The uniforms gave very little protection against the elements during harsh winter temperatures, and no comfort in hot and dry, dusty camps in summer. In the summer of 1864, one Confederate soldier likened a walk through camp to a stroll through an ash heap. "One's mouth will be so full of dust that you do not want your teeth to touch one another." A cannoneer wryly remarked that whenever a grasshopper jumped up, it raised such a cloud of dust that Union lookouts reported that the Confederate army was on the move again. The dust blew through holes in their worn clothing and caked to the sweat on their bodies. "I have no seat in my pants," lamented a Virginian, "the legs are worn out, have had but one pair of socks which are worn out completely, my shirt is literally rotted off me." A new issue shirt proved to be so louse-ridden that he could not bear to wear it.

Clothing deteriorated badly, and there were frequently no reissues, so that by the end of the war uniforms as such had ceased to mean anything. The men simply redressed themselves with whatever they could find to hand.

The Confederate soldier was also poorly equipped with handguns and longarms. At the start of the war, the army had control of only a few of its own armaments manufacturing facilities. It developed more during the course of the conflict, but it was always limited by lack of production equipment and skilled manpower, as well as by the scarcity of materials. As a result, the CSA had to use a mixture of whatever weapons it could find at the beginning of the war: new manufacture of antiquated flintlock and percussion designs and of a few new designs of its own, weapons captured from Union forces, and a small number of imports, especially from Great Britain. In an era of enormous technological inventiveness, Southern manufacturers did play their part, both by

CONFEDERATE INFANTRY EQUIPMENT
1 1st Sergeant's frock coat
2 Forage cap
3 Linen havelock
4 Trousers for 1st Sergeant's frock coat
5 Uniform vest for 1st Sergeant's frock coat and trousers
6 Shirt
7 Cartridge box
8 Cap box
9 Fayetteville rifle
10 Brogans
11 Wooden canteen, name of owner inscribed
12 Haversack
13 Model 1860 Colt Army revolver and holster
14 Side knives

developing new pistol and rifle designs and ingeniously copying those of their foes.

As well as the variable nature of the soldiers' weapons, the army also initially had problems with their troops' abilities to fire the guns. Observers often wondered just who stood to suffer the greater damage from them. Despite their variety, almost all of the muzzle-loading weapons required precisely the same routine from the soldier, a routine which was reduced to a dozen commands and twenty specific motions. At the command "Load," the soldier stood his rifle upright between his feet, the muzzle in his left hand and held eight inches from his body, at the same time moving the right hand to his cartridge box on his belt. At "Handle Cartridge," the paper-wrapped powder and bullet were brought from the box, and the powder end placed between the teeth. The next two commands brought the cartridge to the muzzle, poured the powder into it, and seated the ball in the bore. "Draw Rammer" elicited the appropriate action, and "Ram" sent the bullet down the bore to sit on the powder charge. Another command replaced the rammer, then came "Prime." The soldier brought the weapon up and extending outward from his body with his left hand, while with his right he pulled

LEFT: TROOPER, SUSSEX LIGHT DRAGOONS, CSA
While cavalry uniforms in the Confederacy were more informal than in the other services, still the outfit of the Sussex Light Dragoons was particularly out of the ordinary. They wore a high-topped blue cloth kepi with yellow braid with a brass insignia carrying the letters "S.L.D." Enlisted men wore dark blue trousers and tucked into them a "plastron" paneled shirt front in buff or yellow. Carbine, revolver, and saber completed their outfitting. The origins of the unit are historically obscure, but it probably originated as Company C of the 5th Virginia Cavalry, raised in Sussex County. Its men were later merged into other Virginia cavalry battalions which served in the Army of Northern Virginia under Lee. The unit itself saw little active service, being chiefly stationed in and around Norfolk before being redesignated in the spring of 1862. Their characteristic dress stayed with them throughout their period of war service.

back the hammer to the half-cock position and reached into his cap pouch, removed a cap, and placed it on the nipple.

Now came the real business. "Shoulder": he put the rifle to his right shoulder. "Ready": he took the proper foot stance and returned the piece to a vertical position at his right side, his right hand on the lock, his thumb pulling the hammer back to full-cock. "Aim": up went the rifle to his right shoulder, his head to the butt so that his eye could sight between the opened "V" notch at the rear and over the blade sight at the muzzle. His finger sat ready on the trigger. "Fire": and he did.

However, these guns were more often than not just a lot of smoke and noise. Some officers actually declined to issue to their men live cartridges during skirmish drill, for fear of the mishaps that almost inevitably followed.

A common problem came with the second shot. Amid the shouting and firing, most men

were not conscious of the sound of their own rifle firing, nor of the kick against their shoulders when they did. Consequently, thousands improperly reloaded their weapons – forgetting to bite off the end of the paper cartridge before ramming it home, or else neglecting to place a percussion cap on the firing nipple – and when they pulled their triggers they did not notice that their guns had failed to discharge.

Occasionally, this oversight led to a situation in which the gun could be more dangerous to friend than to foe. After the three-day Battle of Gettysburg in July 1863, the victorious Federals retrieved 27,500 rifles from the battle lines, most if not all of them dropped by the wounded and the killed. Nearly half of them were found to hold two unfired rounds in their barrels. Between three and ten loads crammed the breeches of another 6,000. And one rifle was filled almost to the muzzle with no fewer than twenty-three cartridges.

CONFEDERATE CAVALRY ARTIFACTS
1 Battleflag
2 Slough hat with star insignia
3 Reins and bit
4 Model 1859 McClellan saddle
5 Girth
6 Model 1859 Sharps carbine
7 Haversack
8 Shell jacket
9 Canteen
10 Gauntlets
11 Carbine cartridge box
12 Model 1849 cavalry saber
13 Pair of field glasses
14 Saddlebags
15 Remington New Army revolver complete with holster and percussion caps
16 Pouch for percussion caps
17 Federal officer's sword belt
18 Pair of spurs
19 Leather high riding boots

CHAPTER SEVEN

THE UNION SOLDIER

When the Civil War began, equipment for the men in blue – while sometimes scarce – was usually plentiful and of standard quality. The Federal forces, of course, started the conflict with the advantage of having the Old Union Army as the basis for their traditions, and for the design of their uniforms and personal equipment. They also had the North's superior industrial resources to call upon for their supply. As a result, the dress and equipment of the Federal soldier tended to be more standardized than that of his counterpart in the Confederate States army, while the basic materials were of a higher quality. Compare, for

ABOVE: Co. A, 7th Illinois Color Guard, armed with Henry repeating rifles, far superior to any longarm the Confederates could field. The war may have ended earlier had the weapon been more widely adopted.

example, the overcoat shown at item 12 on page 79 with the Confederate equivalent shown at item 1 on page 75.

There were, of course, exceptions to such uniformity, particularly in the early days of the war when men joined the army from the state militia system that practically encouraged individuality of uniforms and equipment. The results were often multi-colored, brocaded, plume-bedecked costumes that were taken extremely seriously by the wearers, but which may have appeared comical to onlookers. The common soldier and his officers were quick to recognize that bright, colorful attire attracted enemy attention, which was frequently followed by hostile fire. The realities of war, therefore, soon relegated such dress to the footlocker, ceremonial events, the band or home guard.

While such extravagances rapidly diminished in popularity, nevertheless the branch of service of an individual soldier was shown by colored piping and the badges of rank, and this continued throughout the war, although there were variations. The basic colors were red for artillery, blue for infantry, and yellow for cavalry.

By 1863 the Federal infantryman had an adequate supply of good uniforms and sound equipment. As in all armies, Billy Yank still had to cope with shoes that did not fit and which wore out too quickly with all the marching, with wool uniforms that were either one size too large or (even worse) one size too small, which were too warm in the summer, too soggy in the

wet. But only the more remote units had real trouble replacing essential pieces of equipment or uniform. Those that served with the Army of the Potomac in the Eastern theater received far greater regularity in clothes and equipment than their Western compatriots, who were often ragged and reliant on captured Confederate supplies for replacements.

Standard infantry uniforms in the East comprised dark blue frock coat and light blue trousers, plus a blue cloth hat, and Jefferson Brogan style boots. The frock coat was single-breasted and its skirt extended halfway to the knee. It was normally cut raw at the hem of the skirt, and only the upper body was lined. As with other equipment, there were variations, the most common being the shell jacket or "roundabout." Originally derived from the frock coat that had had the skirt removed, this evolved into a specific garment. Reflecting its origins, this short jacket had nine buttons

UNION CAVALRY ARTIFACTS
 1 Carbine cartridge box
 2 Metal curry comb
 3 6th Pennsylvania lance
 4 Cavalryman's gauntlets
 5 Cavalryman's shell jacket
 6 Forage cap
 7 Double-breasted overcoat
 8 Picket rope
 9 Rubber blanket
10 Regulation US Army saddle
   with blanket roll
11 Shoulder sling for a carbine
12 Rolled overcoat
13 Saber belt
14 Pair of field glasses and case
15 Bugler's shell jacket
16 Saddle bags
17 Model 1860 Spencer carbine
18 Model 1860 saber
19 Curb bit and reins
20 Girth
21 Saddle blanket
22 Bugle
23 Farrier's pocket knife

down the front and two on each cuff.

The fatigue jacket was also worn, being described as a four-button "sack" coat. It was originally issued as the soldier's working jacket along with the frock coat for more formal occasions, but as the war progressed it became the soldier's standard coat, replacing the frock coat.

As specified in Regulations for the Uniform and Dress of the Army of the United States – 1861, the standard headgear was the "Hardee" hat. It was made of black felt with a crown six and a quarter inches in height and a brim of three and a quarter inches wide, turned up on one side. The forage cap had originally been issued alongside the Hardee as a working cap. It was similar to the kepi, but had a high welted pasteboard crown. There was a prevalence of non-regulation headgear, however, many soldiers wearing hats that had been "foraged," privately purchased, or supplied from home. Soldiers in Western units favored a brimmed hat to fend off the heat of the sun or torrential rain.

Variations on the standard issue uniforms were wide. Men of the Veteran Reserve Corps, for instance, wore uniforms of sky blue kersey, with dark blue cap and trimmings, the jacket cut short in the cavalry pattern, even though

LEFT: CORPORAL, ILLINOIS CAVALRY

Everything about the cavalryman of the Union seemed to denote color and excitement. His short blue wool shell jacket, gaily trimmed in yellow to denote the mounted service, stood out above his sky blue pants, all of it framed and trimmed by the polished black leather of his belt, boots, shoulder belts and black-trimmed blue kepi. While there were many variations, especially among privately raised and militia groups from prewar days, most Yankee troopers looked like this cavalryman from Illinois. They rode on the same McClellan style saddle, carried the same regulation saber, wore the same Colt .44 Model 1860 Army pistol and, if they were fortunate, carried the same Spencer carbine repeater. Even their spurs were regulation issue, though the fitness of their horses varied widely. All they could not be issued was experience in combat, and that they would have to learn for themselves with a little help from Johnny Reb.

they were strictly an infantry service. The Corps was formed in 1863 in an attempt to place less able-bodied men in some postings away from the front line so as to free the fitter men for active service. Another example was the 7th New York National Guard (also called State Militia), whose men were called "graybacks" for their light gray, short shell jackets and kepis with black trim. The 7th dated back to 1806, its membership composed of the cream of New York City society who paid for their own uniforms and equipment. It was one of the first units to arrive in the relief of Washington in April 1861, following the crisis of Fort Sumter.

One of the most distinctive units, in terms of variation at least, was the 79th New York Infantry, the "Highlanders," formed in 1859 entirely of Scots immigrants and modeled after the 79th Cameron Highlanders of the British Army. When the Civil War broke out its numbers were swelled with English, Irish, and other foreign-born men, but its dress would remain distinctly Scottish. In full dress the men wore kilts, a doublet, sporran, hose, garters, and silver-buckled shoes – and thus were much ridiculed by other regular units. In the field, however, they quickly changed to light blue trousers, or Cameron tartan pants, dark

RIGHT: PRIVATE, 56TH US COLORED INFANTRY
It was inevitable that the Union government would find a way to take the ex-slaves, whose cause had been so great a part in starting the war, and turn them into a weapon for winning it. Thousands wanted to take up arms to fight for their brothers still in bonds in the Confederacy, and eventually several tens of thousands were enlisted in more than 100 all-black regiments; though at the beginning they were regarded more as laborers than combat soldiers. The uniforms and equipment for these units was virtually the same as that for this private of the 56th United States Colored Infantry, and in fact no different from that of the average white soldier. Dark blue wool jacket, light blue wool trousers, blue cloth kepi, Springfield rifle and accompanying bayonet were all standard issue. Most glaringly different was the fact that for most of the war, until at least 1864, black soldiers were paid less than their white counterparts.

blue blouses, and regulation kepis which replaced the Glengarry cap with its checkered border.

The armies of North and South initially fielded recruits who came into the camps carrying all sorts of longarms, including shotguns, hunting rifles and fowling pieces, caplocks, flintlocks, muzzleloaders and new breechloaders, single-shot and repeaters, pop-guns barely big enough to kill a squirrel, and mammoth .69 and .75 caliber "smoke poles." They also looked to arms purchased from Europe to fill their needs, since the American armories needed time to gear up for production. Pretty soon, though, both governments settled down to two basic and favored shoulder arms, the U.S. Springfield Rifle – in one of several variations – and the British-made Enfield. The Springfield in particular became the workhorse weapon of the Union Army, with 1,472,614 of them purchased on contract by the War Department in Washington. along with 428,292 Enfields. Together, they tallied almost three times the combined numbers of all other shoulder arms purchased by Washington.

LEFT: "BUMMER," ARMY OF THE TENNESSEE, USA
For all the differences between the Billy Yanks of the Eastern Theater and those of the West, no soldier was so distinctive to his army and region as the lean, hardened, ever resourceful "bummer" of the Army of the Tennessee. His uniform may have been the same as that of his Eastern counterparts, but it showed in the hundreds more miles he marched, the greater the variations of climate and weather he endured, and the increased uncertainties of re-supply available to this highly mobile army. Chief among these differences was the battered wide-brimmed hat he wore, as opposed to the ubiquitous kepi worn in the Army of the Potomac, and the fact that he traveled light, his kit reduced to the essentials; anything else he needed he could get from the land, a method of soldiering he became expert at. From Tennessee to North Carolina men such as this would take it upon themselves to destroy the heart of the Confederacy.

RIGHT: Men of Company K, 3rd New Hampshire Regiment, relax with their pipes and playing cards outside their "A" tent, which was originally designed for four men, but frequently had to house more.

UNION INFANTRY EQUIPMENT
1 Hardee hat
2 Infantryman's overcoat
3 Neck stock
4 Forage cap
5 Soft knapsack
6 2nd Corps Headquarters flag
7 Model 1840 Non-
   commissioned Officer's
   sword and shoulder belt
8 Enlisted man's shoulder
   scales
9 .69 caliber cartridge box
10 Haversack
11 Model 1858 covered canteen
12 Brogans
13 Sack coat
14 Infantryman's uniform
   trousers
15 Model 1842 sighted musket
16 Infantry accouterments:
   belt, cap box, bayonet, and
   scabbard, cartridge box
17 Soft knapsack
18 Soft knapsack

THE LEADERS

ABOVE: A consummate improviser, the ultimate victor of the conflict, General Ulysses S. Grant, conducts a council of war on the road. Here he is shown leaning over the pew at left, conferring over a map with Meade.

CHAPTER EIGHT

HEROES ALL

ABOVE: One of the premier field commanders of all time, Lee kept a very small staff, and did not utilize it well, doing most of his staff work himself, as had generals in past wars. They called him "the tycoon."

Out of a nation torn in two, and out of a prewar military that was practically non-existent, tens of thousands of leaders, from the mightiest generals to the most obscure lieutenants, virtually appeared out of the crowd. Where they came from, how they learned – and at times failed to learn – the skills necessary to lead men into the inferno, and how they dealt with the sudden power and responsibility given them, have been largely overlooked.

When simple men are called forward by great events, sometimes remarkable things happen. Many of these young men – and many who were not so young – put aside their civilian lives, their educations, loves, and all their other hopes and dreams of the future, to set forth on the great adventure of their generation.

Yet mere participation hardly guaranteed that a man would rise to command. That required something else entirely. A few of them, North and South, had to learn not just how to be leaders, but how to be generals, when the full weight of command both practical and moral would settle upon a single man's shoulders. There was a great deal more to leadership in the Civil War than scene after scene of stirring command and bravery, as thousands of American men were to discover.

GENERAL ROBERT E. LEE

If ever a man was born to be a hero, it was Robert E. Lee. Born January 19, 1807, in Westmoreland County, Virginia, he was the son of a hero, "Light Horse Harry" Lee of the Revolution, and a descendant of one of the "First Families" of the old Dominion. Being a Virginian would dominate his life.

He entered the United States Military Academy in 1825, and graduated second in his class in 1829, to spend the next 36 years in uniform. Lee saw wide and varied service, but it was in combat that he excelled. In the war with Mexico he served on the staff of General Winfield Scott, performing dangerous scouting missions that were integral to American successes. Peacetime found Lee in quieter roles, including superintendent at West Point, though in October 1859 he commanded the contingent that fought and captured John Brown's raiders

at Harpers Ferry. In 1861 Lee had the opportunity for high command with the Union, but with Virginia's secession he followed her fortunes. Briefly he commanded the state militia until President Davis commissioned him a brigadier, and later a full rank general. But Lee's Civil War did not start well. He failed in a command in western Virginia, then commanded the defenses of South Carolina, and by early 1862 was stuck as military advisor to the president in Richmond.

When Joseph E. Johnston fell wounded at Seven Pines in May, Lee got his chance. Davis gave him the command of what would become the Army of Northern Virginia, and the general and the army were never apart for the rest of the war or posterity. In a dazzling campaign Lee drove the Federals away from Richmond, then struck north, defeating them on the old

PERSONAL POSSESSIONS OF GENERAL ROBERT E. LEE
1 Field tent (a mock up)
2 Saddle blanket
3 Scarf (gift from England)
4 Frock coat
5 Frock coat
6 Leather haversack
7 Leather gauntlets
8 Virginia State sword belt
9 The camp bed and blanket used at siege of Petersburg
10 Mess gear utensils
11 Leather riding boots
12 Wooden camp chest
13 Mess gear chest
14 Modified Grimsley saddle
15 Field glasses and case
16 Hat given by General Lee to the Reverend J. Clay Stiles
17 Colt Model 1851 Navy
18 The pen used to sign the surrender at Appomattox
19 A table used at the winter headquarters, 1863-4

Manassas battlefield before launching his first invasion of the North, ending at Antietam. Despite that setback, Lee inflicted a severe defeat at Fredericksburg in December, and the next May, at Chancellorsville, won the most crushing battlefield victory of the war. Elated with his success, he gambled on another invasion, but was stopped at Gettysburg in July.

The spring of 1864 pitted Lee against a new antagonist, U.S. Grant, and only Lee's tactical brilliance prevented Union numbers from pushing him aside. At the Wilderness and Spotsylvania, the North and South Anna, and Cold Harbor, Lee repeatedly stymied Grant, who nevertheless kept coming. By June Lee had his back to Richmond, and no alternative but to accept being besieged. For the next ten months he held Grant at bay, but in early April all the options were gone. Lee and his army made a dash to the west, but Grant caught them at Appomattox, and there on April 9, 1865, Lee surrendered.

Lee spent his last years trying to rebuild his Virginia and discourage sectional enmity. He took the presidency of the failing Washington College at Lexington, and built it into a fine institution, later to be Washington and Lee University. He died in Lexington October 12, 1870, and was mourned in the North and the South as a symbol of dignity and conciliation.

RIGHT: GENERAL ROBERT E. LEE AND LIEUTENANT GENERAL T. J. JACKSON
Interestingly, the great leaders of the war, though professional soldiers, still tended to take a lackadaisical attitude toward their uniforms and toward uniform regulations in general. Robert E. Lee, though the third highest ranking Confederate general in seniority, rarely appeared in anything other than the uniform of a colonel. While regulations prescribed a wreath around three stars for a general's collar, he wore only the stars, and no cuff braid.

His great subordinate, Stonewall Jackson, was only a little more cognizant of regulations. He often appeared in the field in his old U.S. Army jacket and cap from his Mexican War days. At least, when in Confederate uniform, he did wear the proper insignia. Interestingly, in this war the more concerned a general was about the exactness of his uniform, the less able he usually was on the battlefield.

LT. GEN. THOMAS J. JACKSON

Only Robert E. Lee himself has attracted more reverence than his most famous lieutenant, the man called "Stonewall." So great is his hold on the American imagination, that he is the only Confederate general who, some believe, had his life been spared, might have changed the outcome of the war.

He came from the humblest beginnings. Born January 21, 1824, in Clarksburg, Virginia, he was left an orphan by his father's early death, and was raised by a cold and unloving uncle. Secured an appointment to West Point in 1842, he struggled at his studies, mastering by rigorous rote. When he graduated in 1846, he ranked a respectable 17th in his class, and almost immediately went off to war in Mexico, where he performed well in battle. The years after the war proved disappointing, however, and in 1851 he resigned to take a position as a professor at the Virginia Military Institute at Lexington.

Lexington would be his home for the rest of his life. A devout Presbyterian, and an uninspired teacher, he succeeded by determination, just as at West Point. His students ridiculed him, and one allegedly tried to kill him, yet most left the VMI with a grudging respect for the man they called "Tom Fool." Jackson was no secessionist, nor was he passionately attached to slavery, but when Virginia seceded in April 1861 he followed his state into the Confederacy.

What followed is the stuff of legend. After a brief period drilling recruits in Richmond, he was commissioned a brigadier and assigned command of the 1st Virginia Brigade. He led them at the First Battle of Manassas, or Bull Run, and there they both earned an immortal sobriquet when another Confederate general likened their stand in battle to that of a stone wall.

Promotion came quickly and, as Major General Jackson, Stonewall led his command back to the Shenandoah where in the spring of 1862 his combination of lightning movement and deft strategy defeated three separate Union forces greater than his own. He fought with Lee in the Seven Days Battles, and then in August won a considerable victory at Cedar Mountain on his own. At Second Manassas he set up Lee's victory, then fought at Antietam and Fredericksburg, by now a lieutenant general commanding the II Corps of Lee's army.

His greatest day, and his last, came on May 2, 1863, at Chancellorsville, where he led his corps in a wide flanking march around the Union right, and struck a stunning surprise blow that put a whole Federal corps to rout. But accidental shots from his own men left him seriously wounded. Eight days later he died of complications. When he was buried in Lexington, much of the hope of the Confederacy was buried with him.

ABOVE: Thomas J. Jackson in his uniform as a first lieutenant in the Mexican War. A simple instructor at the Virginia Military Institute, he little expected greatness.

LEFT: Lieutenant General Thomas Jonathan "Stonewall" Jackson was only one of many Rebel leaders with numerous family connections in the army of the Confederacy; his included two brothers-in-law who were also generals.

PERSONAL MEMORABILIA OF GENERAL THOMAS JONATHAN JACKSON

1 Confederate forage cap worn during the war
2 Handmade embroidered scarf presented by an admirer
3 Cased Adams revolver with accouterments
4 Leather case for 5
5 Field glasses
6 Forage cap worn by General Jackson
7 A Lefaucheaux Brevete revolver presented to the general by his officers
8 A pair of epaulettes worn on dress occasions at V.M.I.
9 Pair of gold spurs presented to General Jackson by the ladies of Baltimore, Maryland
10–12 Packets of five Le Mat revolver cartridges
13 Leather gauntlet worn by Jackson on the night of his mortal wounding, May 2, 1863, Chancellorsville, Va
14 A pair of silver spurs worn during the war
15 Leather haversack
16 Gold watch carried by General Jackson at Chancellorsville
17 Spur worn at the time of his wounding
18 Jackson's sword: a U.S. Model 1850
19 The black waterproof worn by General Jackson at the moment of his wounding

MAJ. GEN. J. E. B. STUART

There were stories that he grew a beard to conceal a weak chin, rumors countered by his teenage nickname "Beauty." Certainly he stopped female hearts when he rode by in his black hip boots, wearing his plumed hat, and with his saber jangling, followed by that jolly and dashing retinue that included an enormous Prussian and a diminutive banjo player. By that time "Beauty" was long gone, replaced by a single syllable that was known universally, North and South... Jeb.

He was a Virginian, which alone won him many a heart. Born February 6, 1833, he was named James Ewell Brown Stuart to honor several family connections, and secured an appointment to the United States Military Academy, from which he graduated in 1854 with standing sufficient to gain a commission in the cavalry. From then until the outbreak of war he served mainly in frontier duty in Kansas

RIGHT: A pre-war photograph of a man destined to achieve greatness as a Confederate. James Ewell Brown Stuart was obscure as a cavalry lieutenant – as Lee's Jeb Stuart, he became immortal.

facing Indians, and was wounded by an arrow in one hot skirmish. By sheer chance, he was in the east in October 1859, serving temporarily as aide to Colonel Robert E. Lee of the 2nd United States Cavalry, when they were ordered to put down the John Brown raid at Harpers Ferry. Stuart himself led the assault that finally broke into Brown's fort, and was one of the first inside.

Like Lee, Stuart chose to go with Virginia when she seceded, and immediately received command of the 1st Virginia Cavalry, which he led at the First Battle of Bull Run, a performance that won him promotion to brigadier general two months later. The early association with Lee paid off the next spring when Lee took command of the Army of Northern Virginia and he ordered Stuart to reconnoiter the Yankee army on the Peninsula. Stuart rode entirely around the enemy, gaining valuable intelligence and putting a fright into the always timid McClellan, and Lee rewarded him with command of all the army's cavalry, which Stuart would hold until his death.

He proved to be an almost ideal cavalryman, a team player who worked well within the chain of command despite occasional outbursts of adventuring. As a major general he harassed enemy armies, gathered vital intelligence for Lee, and created a legend of dash and daring. He helped win the Second Manassas Campaign, performed ably in the invasion of Maryland, and at Chancellorsville in May 1863 actually took command of the Second Corps after the wounding of Stonewall Jackson.

Stuart met his first real check at Brandy Station in June 1863, when he was surprised and almost defeated by Federal horse. In the Gettysburg Campaign he did not live up to Lee's expectations entirely, but the fault was as much Lee's as Stuart's. Certainly Lee never lost any confidence in the young cavalryman, and when Stuart was mortally wounded at Yellow Tavern on May 11, 1864, dying the next day, Lee was stunned, as was the Confederacy.

LEFT: MAJOR GENERAL J. E. B. STUART

Though hardly as showy as the Yankee General Custer, Rebel Major General Jeb Stuart represented much of what was most dashing in the bold cavaliers of the South. His short jacket, buttoned back in the Revolutionary War style to show its buff facings, the ostrich plume in his hat, the gleaming black high-topped boots were all the trademark of the officer that friends called "Beauty." Most elegant of all were his whiskers, and the merry twinkle in his eyes that everyone around him noted.

Carrying his heavy dragoon saber and his French Le Mat pistol, Stuart could always be found in the middle of the action on any field of battle. Only death from a mortal wound at Yellow Tavern could stop him, and his absence left a permanent gap at the once-merry campfires of the cavalry corps of the Army of Northern Virginia. Even his personal banjo player never quite sounded the same after Jeb Stuart's death.

PERSONAL POSSESSIONS AND MEMORABILIA OF GENERAL J. E. B. STUART

1 Headquarters flag, First National Pattern
2 Stuart's field glasses and case. After his wounding at Yellow Tavern, May 11, 1864, the general gave these to his aide-de-camp Lt. Theodore S. Garnett
3 Stuart's haversack
4 Leather riding boots
5 1858 McClellan saddle
6 Buckskin gauntlets
7 General's silk sash worn by Stuart at Yellow Tavern
8 Stuart's jacket
9 Stuart's wool vest with Federal staff officer's buttons
10 Plumed felt officer's hat, made in Paris
11 Stuart's trousers
12 Field glasses and case
13 Uniform frock coat, possibly Stuart's
14 Whitney revolver carried by Stuart at Yellow Tavern
15 Le Mat 1st Model revolver
16 English holster for 15
17 Tin wash basin and bowl
18 Tin cup
19 Leather gun case
20 Calisher and Terry carbine
21 Model 1860 cavalry saber, of French make
22 Model 1851 Federal saber belt with plate
23 Federal officer's sword belt and plate worn by Stuart at Yellow Tavern

BRIG. GEN. JOHN HUNT MORGAN

General Morgan was born in Huntsville, Alabama, on June 1, 1825. He saw service in the Mexican War, and after discharge from the Army he entered the family business in Lexington, Kentucky, becoming active in the local militia unit, the Lexington Rifles. At the outbreak of the Civil War he took his small unit to Bowling Green and offered his services to General Buckner. Dashing and colorful, he was soon promoted to colonel of the 2nd Kentucky Cavalry and proceeded to establish himself as one of the most feared Confederate cavalry leaders. His raids into Kentucky, Tennessee, Ohio, and Indiana caused great concern to the Federals.

In the summer of 1863 Morgan led his cavalry across the River Ohio and into Indiana and Ohio. Quickly, the Federals were on his trail, and on July 26 they brought Morgan and a few hundred of his men to a halt, forcing them to surrender. On August 1 he was sent to the Ohio State Penitentiary at Columbus, where he was searched and had pocket knives and other useful articles confiscated. But in late November Morgan escaped with a few other prisoners. In a well-thought-out plan that involved tunneling through the foundations into an open yard beyond, Morgan switched places with his also-incarcerated brother, Col. R. C. Morgan, who was on the ground floor of the prison, scaled a high wall, walked to a station and boarded a train that rode through the night to Cincinnati. He took a ferry across the Ohio to his native Kentucky, and from there worked his way south to Tennessee and friendly lines.

In September 1864, while en route to attack Federal units at Knoxville, he was surprised by Federal cavalry and killed.

GENERAL ULYSSES S. GRANT

He was a man who failed at almost everything, but when he found the one thing he could do well, he did it perhaps better than anyone else of his time.

He was born Hiram Ulysses Grant at Point Pleasant, Ohio, on April 27, 1822. Through friends his father secured him an appointment to West Point, but an error led to his name being mistaken as Ulysses Simpson Grant, a change that he found it simpler to adopt than to correct. Grant excelled only in horsemanship, despite which he was placed in the infantry. In the war with Mexico, he served in Zachary Taylor's army in the 4th United States Infantry, and then under Winfield Scott, and saw action that won him plaudits and promotion.

The peacetime that followed found Grant at a Pacific coast outpost, depressed and lonely, and finding solace in drink. He resigned in 1854 and then tried a succession of trades, and failed at all of them. Then came the war, and he offered his services to the governor of Illinois. In June he was commissioned colonel of the 21st Illinois Regiment, then in August he was made a brigadier. He commanded at Cairo, Illinois, and then occupied Paducah, Kentucky, in September. His first battle came in November with a brisk skirmish at Belmont, Missouri.

In February 1862 he moved his growing command to capture Forts Henry and Donelson, opening up most of Tennessee to the Union and forcing the enemy to evacuate western Kentucky. Despite a surprise at Shiloh in April, he turned it into a victory, and thereafter focused his attention on the capture of Vicksburg and control of the Mississippi. Stymied time after time, he kept on coming, until finally on July 4, 1863, Vicksburg was his. By now he was a major general and the Union's most successful commander, and he continued his progress that fall when he lifted the siege of Chattanooga, then routed Braxton Bragg's army at Missionary Ridge.

Lincoln responded by making Grant a lieutenant general, the first since Winfield Scott, in March 1864. With it came overall command of all Union armies, and thereafter Grant planned the coordinated offensives across the continent. He placed himself with the Army of the Potomac, and largely directed it against Lee at the Wilderness, Spotsylvania, and Cold Harbor, then executed a brilliant crossing of the James River without Lee's knowing it, and narrowly missed taking Richmond and Petersburg. When that failed, he besieged Lee for ten months, and finally surrounded him at Appomattox.

A full four star general at the war's end, Grant went on to become embroiled in Reconstruction politics, then won two terms as president. He left office in 1877, and spent his last years struggling, at one point bankrupt, and fighting a race with cancer to finish his memoirs. He won by a matter of days, and when he died July 23, 1885, he left behind one of the finest military autobiographies of all time.

BELOW: General Grant (standing, fifth from left) with a dozen fellow officers, including (fourth from right) Col. Ely S. Parker, a full-blooded Seneca, who wrote out Grant's surrender demands presented to Robert E. Lee.

UNIFORMS AND PERSONAL REGALIA OF GENERAL U. S. GRANT

1 General's silk sash, embroidered
2 Wool frock coat with insignia of full general, a rank awarded Grant in 1866
3 Leather officer's sword belt with gilt belt plate
4 Wool frock coat made by the John Wanamaker Co., Philadelphia. Button groupings show that it is that of a full general c. 1866
5 Leather binocular case
6 Binoculars from 5
7 See 14
8 Sword in an ivory banded case. The silvered and gilt sword was made by Schuyler, Hartley & Graham, New York, while the gilt and bright blade was made by Collins and Co. in 1862. Also shown are a general officer's sword belt and sash
9 Silver cigar case, engraved with Grant's initials
10 Ivory handled pen commemorating Grant's promotion to lieutenant general in November 1863
11 Shoulder insignia of major general
12 Shoulder insignia of lieutenant general
13 Shoulder insignia of full general of the armies
14 and 7 A pair of major general's dress epaulettes

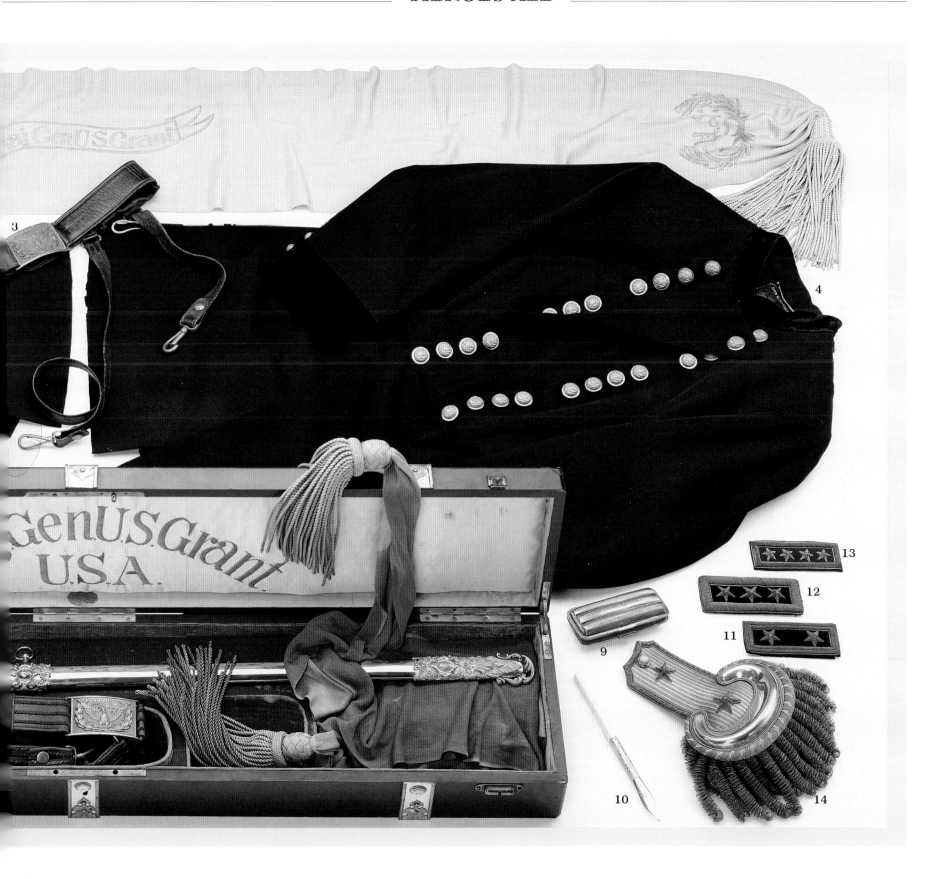

RIGHT: GENERAL-IN-CHIEF U. S. GRANT AND MAJOR GENERAL W. T. SHERMAN Of all the 1,000 and more generals in this war, few if any emerged from greater obscurity to rise to greater heights than these two men. Each a mystery in his way, they became very close friends without ever truly understanding each other. Grant was a simple man of complex instincts who did one thing, and only one thing, really well, and that was winning a war – but he did it better than anyone else. Sherman, by contrast, was far more intelligent, and perhaps something of an intellectual. Yet he was also erratic, excitable, and needed the steadying influence of Grant, who never faltered and never doubted. Together they were the most invincible team Lincoln had and not unlike the magnificent pairing of Lee and Jackson. Each tended to be careless in his uniform. Grant more often than not appeared in the field in a simple private's blouse, with his insignia of rank sewn on.

MAJ. GEN. WILLIAM T. SHERMAN

He may never have said that "war is hell," but few men on either side understood the truth of the phrase so well as the man who "broke hell loose" in Georgia.

Friends called him "Cump." Sherman's father admired the great Shawnee leader Tecumseh, and so honored him by naming his son for him. Born February 8, 1820, at Lancaster, Ohio, young Sherman was orphaned at an early age, and raised by friends, including Senator Thomas Ewing, who got him an appointment to West Point in 1836. In 1840 Sherman finished sixth in his class, but missed the real action in the war with Mexico, being stuck in California where little happened. Slow promotion afterward impelled him to resign in 1853, first for banking in San Francisco, then the law, and finally the superintendency of the Louisiana State Seminary and Military Academy.

Sherman was in Louisiana when the state seceded, and had close friends in the South and a genuine fondness for the region. But his loyalty was to the Union. On May 14 he received appointment as colonel of the 13th United States Infantry, and by summer commanded a brigade in the army beaten at First Manassas. Unlike many, he predicted a long and bloody war. Having performed well in his first battle, he was promoted brigadier in August, and later sent to defend Kentucky. Unfortunately he suffered a minor nervous breakdown, aggravated by exaggerated fears of enemy attack, and the press branded him "crazy Sherman." He quickly recovered, however, and commanded a division under Grant at Shiloh.

Thereafter Sherman's fortunes were linked with Grant's, each a perfect complement to the other. Commissioned a major general in May, Sherman was Grant's right arm for the next year in the operations leading to the capture of Vicksburg. Sherman went with Grant to relieve the siege of Chattanooga in November 1863, conducted his own campaign to Meridian Mississippi that winter, and in the spring of

1864 assumed command of several armies in the western theater and planned and conducted the famous Atlanta Campaign. Thereafter he marched his armies across Georgia and South Carolina to Savannah, cutting the Confederacy in two, and finished the war in North Carolina where he accepted the surrender of the Army of Tennessee.

After the war Sherman succeeded Grant as general-in-chief and four star general, and retired in 1884, thereafter refusing repeated requests to seek the presidency. He wrote his memoirs, one of the finest of their kind, and died February 14, 1891, in New York, one of the most fabled of all American soldiers.

REAR ADMIRAL DAVID FARRAGUT

On a dramatic day in August 1864, one of the Union's mightiest machines of war, the ironclad monitor USS *Tecumseh*, suddenly lurched in the water of Mobile Bay, Alabama, and sank within seconds, taking all but one man aboard to the bottom. She had struck an underwater mine, then called a torpedo. Looking on from his perch in the shrouds of the flagship USS *Hartford*, a native Southerner who had become the Union's greatest naval commander refused to allow the danger of other mines to avert him in his attack on the Confederate fleet awaiting him. "Damn the torpedoes!" he said.

The United States was just twenty-five years and a day old when James Glasgow Farragut was born July 5, 1801 not far from Knoxville, Tennessee. It was a long way to the sea in any direction, but his ferry operator father soon moved to New Orleans for a navy position, and there the Farraguts became closely involved with the family of the famed David Porter, one of the young nation's first naval heroes. After his father's retirement, Farragut became the ward of Porter's son, and with his help won an appointment as a midshipman in 1810. Four years later, Farragut changed his first name from James to David in appreciation.

He would spend the rest of his professional life in the uniform of the United States Navy, winning one plaudit after another. He commanded his first prize ship in the War of 1812 at the age of only 12 years. After the war he served in the Mediterranean, then the West Indies, slowly rising in rank until he settled in Norfolk, Virginia, in 1823, where he married and remained until the outbreak of the Civil War.

In 1861 now a captain, Farragut left Virginia when it seceded and hoped for a significant command, but it was not until January 1862 that he took over the West Gulf Blockading Squadron. He built up the fleet that captured New Orleans in April 1862, and thereafter cooperated in the attack on Vicksburg, meanwhile closing all Confederate ports on the Gulf except Mobile. While his foster brother David Dixon Porter helped Grant take Vicksburg in July 1863, Farragut assisted in the bombardment that led to the surrender of Port Hudson a few days later.

His last great objective was Mobile, heavily defended by forts and Confederate warships. On August 5, 1864, he steamed past the forts, ignored the torpedoes, and captured or dispersed the enemy fleet, with the forts soon sur-

BELOW: David Glasgow Farragut was a heroic navy man through and through, from his service in the War of 1812 to his becoming the United States Navy's first ever vice admiral and, after the war, its first full admiral.

rendering. Lincoln promoted him to vice admiral, the first ever, and two years later Congress created the rank of full admiral for him. The war ruined his health, however, and he died September 30, 1870, still on active duty.

RIGHT: REAR ADMIRAL DAVID FARRAGUT, U.S.N.
The uniform of Union Admiral David G. Farragut was largely patterned after the old prewar United States Navy costume. It was dark blue, with sleeve insignia to show his rank. He also wore the Model 1852 sword and beltplate, a carry-over from prewar service.

Farragut's shoulder straps showed his rank with two stars, with a fouled anchor in between, which denoted that his rank was equivalent to that of a major general in the Army. No other Union naval officer would rise as high as Farragut, and he would become America's first full rank admiral. He was promoted to this high rank on July 25, 1866, and died four years later.

BELOW: After the capture of Mobile Bay, an appreciative public rushed to honor him. Among others, the City of New York provided him with both an elegant home and a beautifully carved presentation sword.

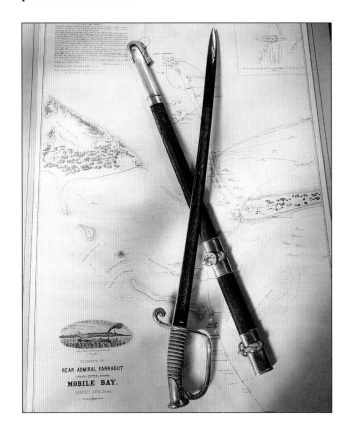

MAJ. GEN. GEORGE H. THOMAS

In an era of nicknames, his rang among the most dramatic. It all came from a September day in 1863, a day in which earlier he had almost panicked and played a role in bringing his army to disaster. But that afternoon he refused to move, and the Confederates could not go around him. That afternoon he became the Rock of Chickamauga.

Ironically he was a native Southerner, born to an old Virginian family on July 31, 1816. When he was 20, old for an entering cadet, George Henry Thomas was appointed to West Point, and finished in 1840 high in his class. His performance won him a commission in the artillery, and he stayed there until 1855, fighting in the Seminole conflict in Florida, and the war with Mexico where he won plaudits and promotion for daring. When the new elite 2nd United States Cavalry was created, Thomas got the plumb position of major, under Colonel Albert Sidney Johnston and Lieutenant Colonel Robert E. Lee, and served in the southwest until the coming of the Civil War.

Thomas bravely decided not to go with his native state when secession came, though it alienated his family from him for the rest of his life. He served first in the Shenandoah Valley, and in August got his general's star and transfer to Kentucky. There at Logan Crossroads, or Mill Springs, he won a small but significant early Union victory that helped collapse his old commander Johnston's Confederate line in Tennessee and Kentucky. He saw action on the second day at Shiloh on April 7, 1862, and won promotion to major general.

Thomas spent the rest of the war in the western theater, first as commander of a division at Perryville and Stones River, and later of a corps in the Army of the Cumberland. At Chickamauga heavy Confederate attacks at first nearly panicked him, and his repeated pleas for reinforcements weakened the center of the Union line just when the Confederates launched a crushing assault. With the army shattered and in retreat, Thomas stood for hours delaying the enemy pursuit, and winning his sobriquet. At Missionary Ridge in November he helped lift the siege of Chattanooga, and in the Atlanta Campaign to follow he commanded his army in Sherman's overall army group. At Franklin and Nashville, Tennessee, at the end of 1864, he all but destroyed the remnant of the Confederate Army of Tennessee in his last actions of the war.

Thomas enjoyed little of peacetime. He commanded in Tennessee during Reconstruction until 1867 and then was transferred to California, dying in San Francisco March 28, 1870. He still remains controversial, championed by some as an unappreciated genius.

ABOVE: Thomas was a sturdy man of large, fleshy build, with a grim set of jaw that betrayed his determined, if plodding, nature. No one ever accused him of flourish, but he was unfailingly dependable, and in a Civil War commander, that was a much to be desired.

RIGHT: Major General George H. Thomas, U.S.A.
There was never anything flamboyant about George H. Thomas. Somewhat more punctilious about uniform than many Yankee commanders, he usually appeared in full regulation attire, as here. He is obviously a major general, his stars just barely visible on his shoulder straps, and the two stars of his rank quite evident on his regulation saddle blanket. His uniform is regulation blue, with yellow belt sash, and a flat-brimmed variation of the old Hardee or "Jeff Davis" hat, with yellow cord.

MAJ. GEN. GALUSHA PENNYPACKER

In a war in which boys became men overnight, one Pennsylvanian with the unlikeliest of martial names became a general even before he was old enough to vote.

He was born near Valley Forge on June 1, 1844, and saddled for life with the name Galusha Pennypacker. He was still just 16 when the war broke out, but he came of a martial heritage, his father a veteran of Mexico and his grandfather of the Revolution, and so young Pennypacker volunteered for the 9th Pennsylvania Infantry, and his company elected him a sergeant. A few weeks later he recruited a new company of his own that became part of the 97th Pennsylvania and elected him its captain, and soon thereafter he was promoted to major, while still only 17.

Pennypacker saw his first real active duty in the forgotten theater of Florida and on the South Carolina coast, including the operations around Charleston in 1863, and the fighting for Battery Wagner. Transferred to Virginia, he and his regiment were with the Army of the James in the fighting at Drewry's Bluff and around Petersburg, and he rose to lieutenant colonel of his regiment in April 1864, and then colonel in command of a brigade in the XXIV Corps in August. In the several assaults in the Petersburg Campaign, Pennypacker was wounded four times, but still recovered to return to duty. He was well liked by his men for his cheerfulness and reliability, even though many of them were some years older than he.

In December and January 1865 Pennypacker went with the Army of the James in the amphibious assault on Fort Fisher, near Wilmington, North Carolina, and in the final successful attack he was dangerously wounded, making a total of eight times that he was hit during the war. He was hospitalized for the rest of the year, but on February 15, 1865, while still only 20, he was promoted brigadier general. In addition to his other honors, Pennypacker later would be awarded the Medal of Honor (today called the Congressional Medal

of Honor), for his service at Fort Fisher, where his commander declared that Pennypacker was the greatest hero produced in the action, and that without him the Yankees might not have captured the fort, thus spelling the doom of Wilmington.

After the war young Pennypacker stayed in the army as colonel of the 34th Infantry and later the 16th Infantry, which he continued to lead until his retirement in 1883, when not yet 40. After leaving the army he returned to Philadelphia, where he died October 1, 1916, a lonely bachelor whose adult years never matched the tremendous excitement of his youth.

LEFT: The youngest general in American history, Galusha Pennypacker was wounded five times during the Civil War, and was awarded the Medal of Honor for conspicuous bravery during the Union action at Fort Fisher. He was appointed general at the age of 20, before he could even vote!

BELOW: U.S. Army Model 1904 Medal of Honor complete with case, belonging to General Pennypacker. The Medal of Honor at this time did not feature the neck suspension ribbon

BOTTOM: U.S. Army Model 1896 Medal of Honor, complete with presentation case.

MAJ. GEN. GEORGE A. CUSTER

A fellow officer once described him as a "circus rider" gone absolutely mad. With his black velvet sailor shirt, long reddish ringlets, and red bandanna, it was obvious to one and all that George Armstrong Custer liked attention.

"Autie," as he was called from youth, was born near Scio, Ohio, December 5, 1839, and dreamed from youth of being a soldier. He grew up with his sister's family, and taught school briefly in the mid-1850s, but West Point was always on his mind. Legend had it that he

RIGHT: Outrageous in dress and demeanor he may have been, nevertheless George Armstrong Custer was a fearless and accomplished cavalry leader during the Civil War, rapidly rising over longer-serving colleagues to become brigadier general.

FAR RIGHT: Colorful and daring, Custer ended the war as major general. Here, posing for a studio portrait, he is shown paying tribute to both his wife for her care and concern, and to another hero believed to be his younger brother, Thomas, who was twice awarded the Medal of Honor during the Civil War, the only soldier in American history so honored.

finally got an appointment to the Military Academy thanks to the influential father of a local girl because he did not appreciate Custer's attentions to his daughter. He entered the academy in 1857 and achieved one of the worst records – short of dismissal – in its history, finishing last in his class in June 1861. Nevertheless, with the war just starting, he was immediately commissioned and sent to the army advancing into Virginia, where he saw his first action at Manassas in July. Somehow Custer got a staff appointment with General George B. McClellan, commanding the Army of the Potomac, and later on with the staff of General Alfred Pleasonton, commander of the army's cavalry.

He was undeniably bold and daring, and for two years showed himself a fearless and useful officer. In the cavalry fight at Aldie, Virginia, on June 17, 1863, he led a portion of Pleasonton's cavalry under orders from the general, and so distinguished himself that on June 29, 1863, with little warning, he was elevated several ranks to brigadier general and given a brigade.

Two days later he led it at Gettysburg, in the cavalry fighting east of the main battlefield, and led it well.

Custer participated in all of the cavalry fighting of the army subsequent to Gettysburg until he was transferred to the Shenandoah in the fall of 1864. There he led a division in battle at Winchester and Cedar Creek, then returned to the Army of the Potomac for the final campaign to Appomattox. Custer's division was instrumental in blocking the path of Lee's retreat, and compelling the surrender.

Though he finished the war a major general, Custer reverted to lieutenant colonel of the new 7th United States Cavalry, and with it his destiny would be linked until he and more than 200 of his men were killed on the Little Big Horn on July 25, 1876. Though his spectacular death always overshadowed his Civil War service, he had been, for all his faults and vainglory, one of the finest of the "boy generals" of the war.

RIGHT: MAJOR GENERAL G. A. CUSTER
The "Boy General," they called him, though there were a few generals on both sides actually younger than George Armstrong Custer. Still, when he became a major general in 1865 at the age of twenty-five, he set a record yet to be broken. Custer was well known in the Army, and could hardly be mistaken thanks to his theatrically flamboyant manner and dress. He virtually designed his own uniform. He wore a dark blue short jacket, with a blue sailor-collar shirt underneath, a red cravat at the neck, blue trousers tucked into oversized cavalier-style black riding boots, and a wide-brimmed hat with his insignia of rank. Easiest to recognize of all was his long, curly blond hair. As a lowly captain, Custer did not stand out from the crowd of officers. With his rise to prominence, he became steadily more theatrical and ostentatious in dress and manner, facts, however, that could not detract from his leadership qualities.

THE GENERALS

ABOVE: Major General Joseph Hooker may not have been the best of the war's generals, but in looks, in daring, and in bravery, he was not unlike the rest. Patriots, poltroons, and everything in between, they gave both color and command to their armies.

THE GENERALS

There are two enduring images that come down to us from the Civil War. One is of the haunting face of a young boy, hardly yet a man, in his new uniform, about to go off to find adventure at war, and quite probably his death on the journey. The other is of the resplendent, bewhiskered general, outfitted in grand military raiment, glittering in medals and finery, strutting before the camera just as he presumably did before his men as he led – or sent – them into battle.

No general of the Civil War more epitomized the color and panoply of war than P.G.T. Beauregard. Here at left are his sword sash, kepi, epaulettes, trousers, and tasseled beret.

Both images are in large part mis-representations, but the misconception of what a Civil War general officer was like is far the more prevalent. From the moment the war started, right down to the present, spectators and students have argued the merits of this general or that, and debated their campaigns as if campaigns and battles were exclusively the expressions of generals' minds. The reality of Civil War generals and generalship is considerably different.

For one thing, there has always been disagreement over just who *was* a general. In the Confederacy, only men formally appointed by President Jefferson Davis can be considered genuine generals, even though many of these did not

subsequently go through the process of formal nomination to and confirmation by the Senate. Yet a host of other men took it upon themselves to adopt the uniform of a general and even to call themselves generals, some holding state militia commissions, and others simply "promoting" themselves. By 1862 there were four grades of general in the Confederate forces: brigadier, major, lieutenant, and full general. However, all wore the same insignia, making it next to impossible to identify a general's rank by his uniform.

Chaos of a different sort reigned among Union generals. For most of the war there were only two grades, brigadier and major general. In 1864 the rank of lieutenant general was reactivated and given to U.S. Grant. However, confusion entered the picture thanks to what were called "brevets," essentially honorary promotions given in recognition of outstanding acts, but which were not recognized for purposes of rank or command. Some 1,367 men were made brevet brigadier and major generals, when their real ranks never exceeded those of colonel, lieutenant colonel, major, and – in a few cases – even captain. Yet when not on the field they could wear the uniform of a general and be addressed as such. Worse, men could hold one rank in the Regular Army and another in the temporary Volunteer service raised for the duration of the war, and brevets in both services! Thus one officer could hold two different ranks in each service, or a total of four different Regular and Volunteer ranks and brevets.

In fact, 583 men genuinely held full rank generalcies for the Blue, while 425 others wore the stars and wreath of a Confederate general on their collars; in all, 1,008. Beneath the stars of every one of them lies a story worth telling.

FACING PAGE: The premier Union general of them all, U.S. Grant, who emerged from absolute obscurity to become the outstanding grand commander of the war. He appears here in the fall of 1864 at Cold Harbor, Virginia, during the Petersburg campaign. **ABOVE LEFT:** Jefferson Davis, president of the Confederacy, kept to himself the prerogative of appointing all generals, with mixed results. **ABOVE:** Abraham Lincoln struggled for years to find the men he needed to lead his armies.

CHAPTER NINE

THE ARMY COMMANDERS

ABOVE: A successful general might be honored with a specially struck medallion, such as this one commemorating George H. Thomas' victory at Nashville in 1864.

Ⓞne of the great myths of the Civil War is that somehow the Confederacy enjoyed a wondrous advantage of talent among its generals at all levels. The truth is quite the opposite, and looking at the highest level of all, the army commanders, one almost has to feel sorry for President Jefferson Davis, considering the woeful lack of talent with which he had to deal.

Eight men held the rank of full general in the Southern armies, all of them professional soldiers in the old pre-war United States Regulars. Yet only three of them would ever have been likely to have risen to that rank had there been no war, and the rest would probably have lived and died as forgotten men, like most of the rest of the junior officers of what was then called the Old Army.

Ironically, the senior general above all others in the Confederate service was a man still virtually unknown. Samuel Cooper was a living anomaly. A native New Yorker who had spent 46 years in uniform when the war broke out, he probably "went South" because of his ties by marriage to Virginia's prominent Mason family. He had been adjutant general in the Old Army, but never actually rose above the rank of lieutenant colonel. But when Davis made him adjutant and inspector general of the Confederacy, he made him a full general with seniority over all others. But Cooper never had led,

LEFT: Gen. George G. Meade, seated at center, was the last, and best, commander of the Army of the Potomac. **BELOW**: Meade's presentation sword, the kind of mark of esteem given to generals who succeeded. **BELOW LEFT**: Samuel Cooper was the highest ranking general in the Confederacy, yet never took the field, and spent his whole war at a desk job in Richmond – a thankless task made worse by Jefferson Davis' constant interference.

and never would lead, troops in the field. He was a desk general from the first day of the war to the last.

Next in seniority to Cooper was Davis' friend and boyhood hero, Albert Sidney Johnston, a real combat veteran from whom everyone expected great things. He had fought in the Black Hawk War, then in the Texas Revolution, where he became general-in-chief, then in the war with Mexico in 1846-48, and after that on the frontier. In 1861 he was a full colonel and brevet Brigadier, and when Davis made him a full general next in seniority to Cooper, he in effect decreed that Johnston should be the premier field commander of the Confederacy. Yet he proved to be largely a failure, and during his brief months in command in the Mississippi Valley the Confederacy lost vital ground that eventually helped lose it the war. When Johnston tried to regain what was lost by his surprise attack at Shiloh on April 6, 1862, he ignored a wound in his leg and allowed himself to bleed to death.

An even more celebrated "might-have-been" among the army commanders was another

ABOVE: The war's first test of generalship came here at First Manassas in 1861. It was as much by accident as design that the Confederate leaders triumphed. Such early battles were the testing grounds for leaders North and South. It proved to be the first and last big command for General Irvin McDowell, the defeated Yankee commander, but it elevated others like Beauregard and Johnston.

Johnston, Joseph Eggleston. A Virginian who had been quartermaster general in the Old Army before the war, he boasted an exalted reputation that his actual record belied. Following his victory at First Manassas in July 1861 – a victory that owed little to his management – he feuded with Davis over his being ranked below Cooper and others, and then proceeded to demonstrate tendencies that dominated his course for the rest of the war: fear of responsibility, unwillingness to communicate with his commander-in-chief, and an unfailing instinct to retreat without fighting. He came perilously close to losing Richmond in the spring of 1862, before a wound fortuitously put him out of action. The next year he played a large role in the bungling that lost Vicksburg, and then when he took command of the

Army of Tennessee at the end of the year he proceeded to fall back continuously, abandoning North Georgia to William T. Sherman in 1864. When he refused to say that he would not give up Atlanta without a fight, Davis relieved him. Yet so powerful were Johnston's friends in Richmond's power circles, and so limited Davis' alternatives, that he restored him to the command in 1865, when Johnston fell back again through the Carolinas, and finally surrendered his army without authority from Davis. However, in spite of his consistently poor performance, Johnston is still hailed as the untried genius of the Confederacy, due largely to his own boastful memoirs and the promotion of his cause by enemies of Davis, who used Johnston as a tool to further their own vendettas. He was, in fact, a timid,

LEFT: First Manassas made Joseph E. Johnston, but for the next four years he consistently failed to live up to his initial promise. Indeed, he would give President Davis almost continual trouble and frustration as he sacrificed one opportunity after another while consistently keeping his president in the dark as to his plans and movements. A man with an excellent brain, Johnston lacked the force of moral courage and the spirit of self-sacrifice that made several lesser men into much greater commanders. He would be himself one of the principal architects of his inflated post-war reputation, based almost solely on his claims of what he "would have done." Based on actual performance, he rates toward the bottom of the Confederacy's full-rank generals.

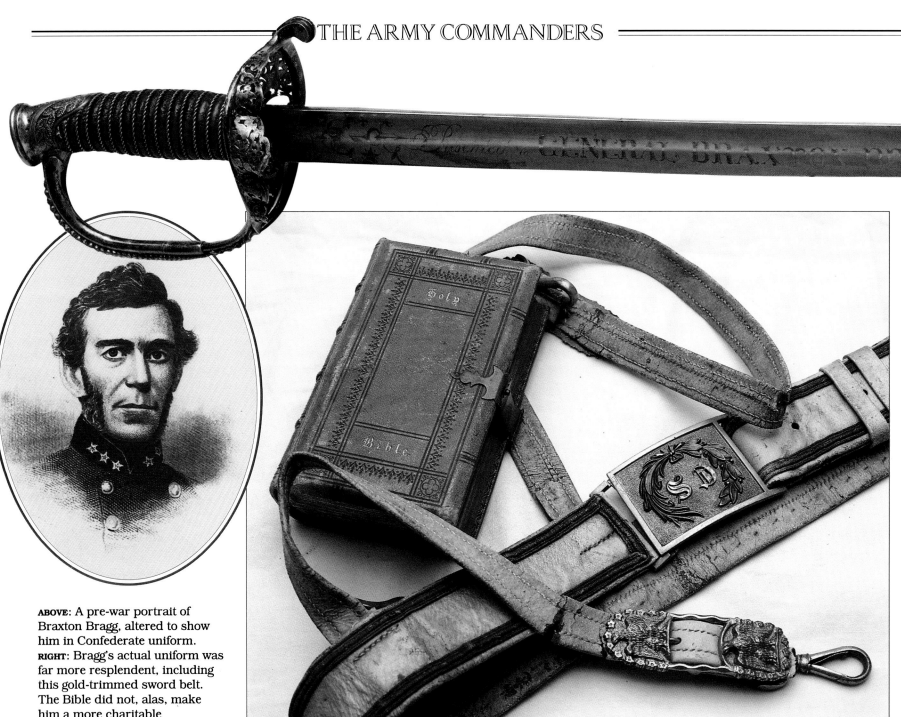

ABOVE: A pre-war portrait of Braxton Bragg, altered to show him in Confederate uniform. **RIGHT**: Bragg's actual uniform was far more resplendent, including this gold-trimmed sword belt. The Bible did not, alas, make him a more charitable commander. **TOP**: Bragg's sword scabbard, simple and unpretentious. **FACING PAGE LEFT AND RIGHT**: Two views of Bragg's uniform blouse, showing the three stars in wreath on the collar, the rows of buttons in pairs, and the four rows of braid on the sleeve, all marks of a general's rank.

quarrelsome officer who lacked the moral courage for high command.

Ironically, the most despised of the Confederacy's high generals, Braxton Bragg, was probably Johnston's superior. He may have been largely incompetent as a battlefield commander, a flawed strategist, and a man so mentally and emotionally ill much of the time that he fought his own generals more than he did the enemy, but at least he was not afraid to commit himself to battle. The problem was that, once in a fight, he could not control it, could not "read" the progress of events to know when he had an advantage to press, or when it was time to withdraw. As a result, he alternately gave up too easily or pressed on, wasting lives when the battle was already lost. At Chickamauga in September

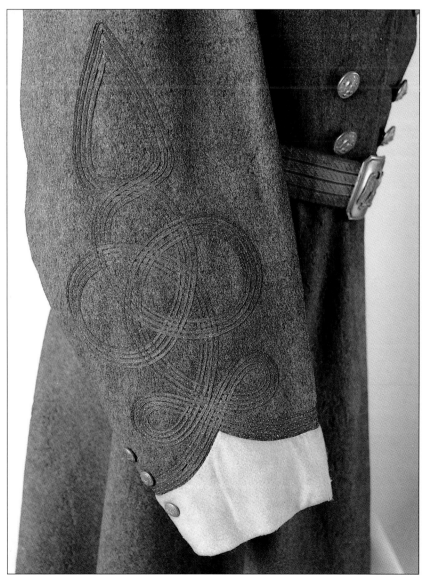

BELOW: "Portici," the Wilmer McLean home at Manassas, headquarters for P.G.T. Beauregard in the only major victory of his Confederate career. **RIGHT:** A part of the Chickamauga battlefield, where Bragg unwittingly won the most stunning Confederate victory of the war. **FACING PAGE LEFT:** The tragic yet heroic John Bell Hood, least able of the major field generals of the Confederacy. He had the heart but not the head for army command. **FACING PAGE RIGHT:** Beauregard. First to last, he was on his own side more than the South's.

1863, he gave the Yankees their most humiliating defeat of the war, then failed to follow it up, and two months later suffered the most humiliating defeat ever inflicted on Southern arms, at Missionary Ridge. Worse, when he lost a fight his first instinct was to place the blame on his subordinates, even if it meant fabricating false charges against them and soliciting perjured testimony.

Of the rest, little need be said. John Bell Hood was made a "temporary" full rank general when he replaced Joseph E. Johnston in command of the Army of Tennessee in July 1864. He proceeded almost to destroy that army by desperate and ill-

conceived attacks around Atlanta, then led it to near-ruin in a campaign into Tennessee that stopped with the debacle at Nashville in December. P.G.T. Beauregard, the hero of Fort Sumter, was at least willing to fight, but he was so wildly impractical in his schemes that they might have resulted in the Confederacy's ruin if carried out. He feuded so venomously with Davis, however, that he never held an important army command after he replaced

BELOW: Edmund Kirby Smith had little claim to being a high commander, yet managed to rise to the top echelon of Rebel generals. More than anything else, he was an administrator and politician in uniform.

RIGHT: Beauregard's uniform blouse shows the fastidiousness of the man himself, perfectly – and somewhat ostentatiously – appointed. The gold braid epaulettes were non-regulation, and worn by very few other generals North or South. The belt plate is unique to Beauregard. **FAR RIGHT:** The blouse of John B. Hood. He, like Beauregard and others, affected buttons in threes, the old U.S. Army pattern for major generals and above, though Confederate regulations did not provide for such usage.

Sidney Johnston briefly following Shiloh. Then there was the most inexplicable of all, Edmund Kirby Smith. He rose no higher than major in the Old Army, but steadily advanced from lieutenant colonel to lieutenant general in only eighteen months, and to full general a further eighteen months later. He never commanded on the field in a major battle, politicked continually behind the scenes for promotion, then evidenced mortal fear of responsibility every time he got it. Only his blatant sycophancy toward Davis can explain his advancement.

In the final analysis, of the Confederacy's army commanders only one was a truly great general – but how great he was! Robert E. Lee dominated Confederate arms then as he does Confederate memory now. Yet at the beginning of the war he almost missed his chance for greatness, for Davis kept him in Richmond as an adviser. Then his first independent command in western Virginia in 1861 ended in failure, and in his next, in South Carolina, his men derisively dubbed him "Granny" Lee and "Spades" Lee. Lee only got his chance when Johnston was wounded in May 1862, but from then on he

LEFT: The Confederacy's one incontestably great army commander sits between his son and his military secretary. Robert E. Lee sat for photographer Mathew Brady just days after his surrender at Appomattox in April 1865, the fire of battle not yet gone from his eyes. No other general in the South took so naturally to army command; no other set such an unmatchable example of selflessness and sacrifice. To the left is his son G.W.C. "Custis" Lee. He started the war as an aide on President Davis' staff, but won a minor field command by war's end. Standing at right is Lieutenant-Colonel Walter Taylor. Lee liked to have bright young officers on his staff, and military secretary Taylor was one of the best. Lee's lack of ostentation is evident in his uniform. No frills, no epaulettes, no braid on his sleeves. Indeed, his collar insignia is that of a colonel, lacking the wreath around the stars. Nor do his trousers show the regulation stripe. It was characteristic of the modesty of the man.

RIGHT: Mute evidence of the brilliance of a Confederate corps commander, T.J. "Stonewall" Jackson. These ruins of the Yankee rail center at Manassas tell of Jackson's out-foxing of Pope, and the high cost in materiel to the Federals. The August 1862 photo is believed to be by master artist Timothy O'Sullivan.

ABOVE: John Pope was the unlucky commander whose first – and last – battle as army commander was against Lee and Jackson. He also had to fight enemies in his rear, not least George B. McClellan, (standing at right). Like Beauregard, "Little Mac" was first and foremost on his own side; like Joseph Johnston, he had neither the courage nor character for command.

showed what he and his immortal Army of Northern Virginia could achieve. Davis lamented that only one great general ever emerged in a generation, and he needed half a dozen. In the end, all he got was Lee, but he proved himself as good as a host.

By contrast, while few of the Union's army commanders demonstrated the brilliance or flourish of Lee, taken as a group they were considerably superior to their Confederate counterparts. Ironically, with a few exceptions, the best known are the failures – perhaps better known because they failed against Lee – and they are therefore inextricably linked with him. Each of them: Irvin McDowell, John Pope, Ambrose Burnside, Joseph Hooker and, most notably of all, George B. McClellan, failed in the face of the great gray chieftain. Interesting enough, such men had near-counterparts in the Confederate high command. McDowell, like Bragg, was brusque, aloof and disliked by his subordinates. Burnside, like Hood, lacked the brains for his position. McClellan, like Joseph E. Johnston, lacked the courage, and was too prone to play politics in the rear. Pope, rather like Beauregard, was bold, but bombastic and impractical. Hooker was at least a good fighter, but top command overwhelmed him and he lost confidence in himself. Every one of them commanded the Army of the Potomac, or major elements of it, against Lee. Only McClellan, at Antietam in September 1862, gained what could be called a victory over him, and even then Lee bested him in a fashion by extricating his army from a trap that a more daring commander might have used to destroy utterly the Confederate army.

LEFT: Affable, likable, somewhat, bumbling, Ambrose E. Burnside looked like a leader, but that was as far as it went. A good organizer on paper, he was inflexible and unimaginative on the field. At Antietam (below), he wasted lives repeatedly trying to cross "Burnside Bridge" under fire, when the creek could have been waded unopposed a few hundred yards away. Following the debacle at Fredericksburg in December 1862, he would turn command of his army over to Joseph Hooker (far left), who would lead it to ruin at Chancellorsville. He simply lost confidence in himself, and thereby gave up the best opportunity any Yankee chieftain ever had to crush Lee decisively.

ABOVE: General George G. Meade, able but unsung commander of the Army of the Potomac, in 1864. ABOVE RIGHT: Meade's uniform, including his blouse, hat, sword belt and sash, kepi and hat, and his beautiful enamel-and-gilt presentation sword. The epaulettes, as usual, were rarely worn. RIGHT: Meade's 1864 headquarters at Globe Tavern, Va.

Not until George G. Meade took command of the Union army in June 1863 did it finally get the commander it needed. He was not dynamic, not flamboyant, not even that likeable to many of his subordinates. But he was unfailingly dependable, unflinching in the face of adversity, and willing to fight. At Gettysburg he gave Lee the worst beating the Army of Northern Virginia ever took in the open field, and he would retain command of the Army of the Potomac until the end of the war, rarely showing brilliance, but an unwavering competence that won the admiration of his superiors and subordinates.

It was from the western theater of the war that the Union's premier army commanders emerged. Not that the region did not also have its share of

FAR LEFT: Abrupt, arbitrary, and a Democrat in a Republican-controlled Union, Don Carlos Buell was disqualified by temperament and politics to last as an army commander. Tactical loser at Perryville, he still forced Bragg out of Kentucky in 1862, but was replaced within weeks amid accusations – unfounded – about his loyalty and charges – well founded – of being too cautious. LEFT: Buell's replacement was the profane, brilliant, Catholic, William S. Rosecrans, veteran of several minor victories, who gained a narrow victory at Stones River, then lost his reputation at Chickamauga a year later when he panicked.

failed leaders. Don Carlos Buell, commanding the Army of Ohio, met defeat by Bragg at Perryville in October 1862, and was so unpopular otherwise that he did not last long at all. More successful was William S. Rosecrans, who showed some capability in 1862 fighting in Mississippi, and thus rose to command of the Army of the Tennessee. He fought Bragg to a stand-off at Stones River, Tennessee, between December 1862 and January 1863, but was then routed by him at Chickamauga, and surrendered his position to a successor once Bragg besieged him in Chattanooga.

ABOVE: General Meade sits in the center looking at the camera, while surrounded by his staff and generals in Virginia in 1865.

BELOW: E.O.C. Ord owed his military rise almost solely to his friendship with U.S. Grant. He took command of Union forces in Richmond when the city fell, and here sits with his daughter on the porch of the Confederate executive mansion.

RIGHT: General George H. Thomas rose to high army command despite being disliked by both Grant and Sherman. But his string of victories put him among the most successful of all Civil War commanders. It cost him the love of his Virginia family, who turned his portrait to the wall and severed all future relations with him.

In Rosecrans' place came one of the great commanders, George H. Thomas, a Virginian who remained true to the Union. He was never brilliant, and was often accused of being too slow and plodding. But when he acted, as when he virtually destroyed Hood at Nashville, he could be devastating. Equally unsung were men who led armies west of the Mississippi, like E.R.S. Canby, who accepted the surrender of two Confederate armies at war's end, and showed promise that opportunity never allowed to develop. More dynamic were men like James B. McPherson, who led the Union Army of Tennessee in 1864 until his untimely death near Atlanta, and who was a favorite with U.S. Grant. Other Grant

cronies like E.O.C. Ord and John M. Schofield also rose to army command for little reason other than Grant's patronage.

Two men above all others rose to the heights thanks partly to Grant, but more so to their own talents. The pugnacious – some would say vicious – little Philip H. Sheridan started the war as an obscure officer in Missouri, but by being in the right place at the right time steadily rose and came to Grant's attention. By 1864 he was a major general given command of a small army in Virginia's Shenandoah Army. Showing a positive jugular

ABOVE LEFT: John M. Schofield, another of the less-than-brilliant men elevated thanks to Grant's patronage. ABOVE: Philip H. Sheridan, a ruthless warmaker who proved a deadly enemy to foes, whether in Gray or Blue. LEFT: E.R.S. Canby, who was destined to fight in the backwaters of the war.

ABOVE: Still a man of controversy after more than a century, William T. Sherman ranks among America's greatest commanders. He had little use for the finery of the army, and was not often seen in his full dress uniform, shown at right, especially with its velvet collar and cuffs.

instinct, he waged a single-minded sort of war to clear the valley of the enemy, and did so with ruthless efficiency.

Even more effective, and probably the most intelligent of all the Union high command, was William T. Sherman. A brigade commander at First Manassas in 1861, he was almost eclipsed when nervous exhaustion practically prostrated him at the end of the year, leading to exaggerated reports that he had lost his mind. Grant saved him, and steadied by the calm, imperturbable guidance of his mentor, the erratically-brilliant Sherman became

Grant's chief lieutenant, rising from corps to army command by 1863, and then in 1864 taking over an army group for the conquest of Georgia. Although never exceptional on the battlefield in tactical command, as an overall theater and group commander he was ahead of his time.

Above them all, however, stood the scruffy, unkempt, nondescript Grant, a pre-war failure at everything. He was not as smart as Sherman, as ruthless as Sheridan, as brilliant on the battlefield as others. But he had the overriding quality of unshakable self-confidence and singleness of purpose. He believed in himself and never turned aside from a goal. His rise to become general-in-chief is a pure American success story, as inexplicable as it later appeared inevitable. He led a mere regiment at the beginning, but was backed by influential politicians and good fortune. Surprised in his first army command at Shiloh, he doggedly stood his ground and turned near-defeat into a qualified victory, then swiftly went on to more victories. When he captured Vicksburg in July 1863 he became the Union's premier hero, and stayed such after he relieved the siege of Chattanooga and went east to become general-in-chief, as a lieutenant general. Inevitably he had to come up against Lee, the best in blue against the best in gray. He matched Lee daring for daring, stroke for stroke, and with the aid of unlimited manpower resources drove the Southern giant back into the heart of Virginia to the very gates of Richmond, there besieging him for ten months until the final, and inevitable, last week, when the armies raced for Appomattox. Outnumbered and outclassed in every sort of material as Lee was throughout the war, it took the coming of Grant to beat him at last.

ABOVE: U.S. Grant. No one expected anything of him at the war's outset. Incredibly, he rose above all the rest to the highest rank in U.S. Army history to that time. He did it by a mixture of daring, sound logic, excellent planning, and what Sherman thought was a simple, unflinching confidence in success. When the war ended he returned to a life dogged by failure. War was the one thing he did well.

—— CHAPTER TEN ——

THE GREAT LIEUTENANTS

ABOVE: Lee's greatest lieutenant, Thomas J. "Stonewall" Jackson. Like Grant, he waged war better than he did anything else, guided by fanatical faith and zeal.

Generals like Grant and Lee did not fight their battles on their own, of course. Indeed, neither of them ever personally led even a squad of soldiers during the war. Their brilliance shone only thanks to their skill in identifying promising subordinates who could take their instructions and translate them into action. It is chiefly among such secondary commanders that the legendary predominance of ability in Confederate gray is to be found. Lee, especially, enjoyed the services of some of the most brilliant lieutenants of the war.

Half of a good subordinate general lay in his commander's ability to "bring him along." None of

the great lieutenants of the war began at high command. To a man they started in 1861 as brigade, regimental, or even company commanders. Attracting attention, usually for their daring, as captains and major and colonels, they were spotted by senior men as officers of promise. As the armies rapidly grew in 1861-62, and as army organization expanded to keep pace, need constantly arose for good men at ever higher levels of command. Thus such men became among the early brigadiers, commanding brigades. By late 1861 or early 1862 they were rising to major general, to lead divisions. And later that year, when both sides officially adopted corps

organization, these men rose again, and in the Confederacy they became lieutenant generals.

No one was better than Lee at the task of spotting a promising officer and bringing him along, though he had the benefit of starting with wonderful material. At the outset, when he took command of the Army of Northern Virginia, he inherited the 41-year-old South Carolinian James Longstreet, one of the solidest corps commanders of the war. In every battle of the war he gave Lee complete satisfaction, with the exception of Gettysburg, and even there his supposed failures are more the invention of his post-war enemies. Lee rarely complained of "my old war horse," as he called Longstreet, and no lieutenant general ever served him better.

While Longstreet led the I Corps of the Army of Northern Virginia from beginning to end, the II Corps would have four commanders in all. At the end of the war, when it was a shattered remnant of

LEFT: Underappreciated by most except Lee, James Longstreet was a most capable corps commander hindered chiefly by contentiousness and a tendency to politic. His biggest mistakes were after the war when he criticized Lee and became a Republican – twin heresies in the South. ABOVE: Longstreet's dreamed-of independent campaign in Tennessee came to nothing with his attack on Knoxville, which ended in his repulse.

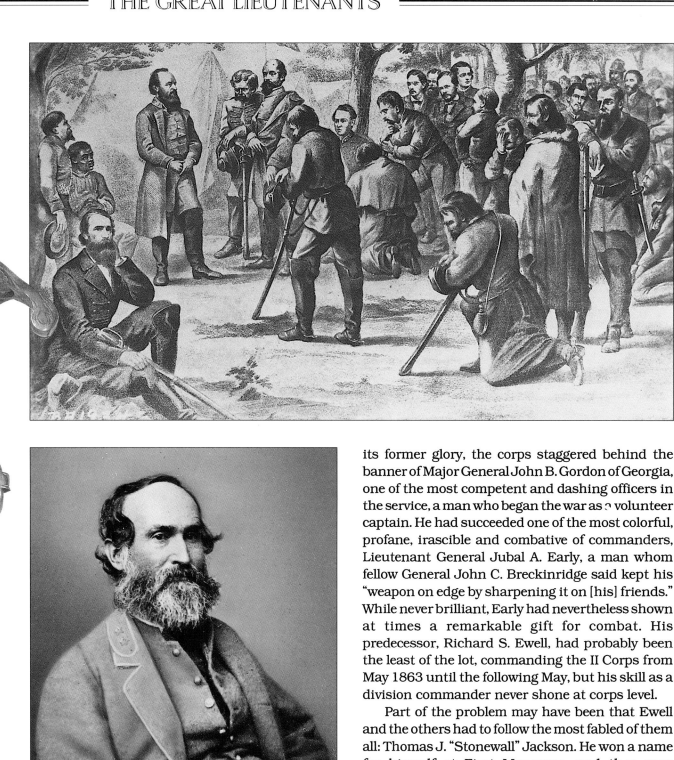

its former glory, the corps staggered behind the banner of Major General John B. Gordon of Georgia, one of the most competent and dashing officers in the service, a man who began the war as a volunteer captain. He had succeeded one of the most colorful, profane, irascible and combative of commanders, Lieutenant General Jubal A. Early, a man whom fellow General John C. Breckinridge said kept his "weapon on edge by sharpening it on [his] friends." While never brilliant, Early had nevertheless shown at times a remarkable gift for combat. His predecessor, Richard S. Ewell, had probably been the least of the lot, commanding the II Corps from May 1863 until the following May, but his skill as a division commander never shone at corps level.

Part of the problem may have been that Ewell and the others had to follow the most fabled of them all: Thomas J. "Stonewall" Jackson. He won a name for himself at First Manassas, and then won legendary status with his Shenandoah Valley Campaign of 1862, defeating three separate Yankee armies with his own under-strength command. Fighting with Lee though the summer and at Antietam, he was put in command of the II Corps

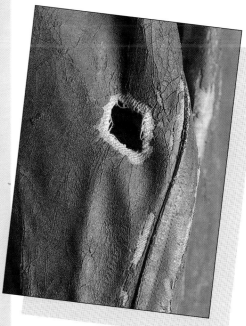

FACING PAGE FAR LEFT: General A.P. Hill's saber, which was with him at his mortal wounding. FACING PAGE TOP: The devoutly religious Jackson sometimes led prayers in his headquarters. He stands at left, A.P. Hill sitting at left and Richard Ewell standing third from the left. FACING PAGE BOTTOM: Jackson's last successor in command of the II Corps, Jubal A. Early was cranky, contentious, and flawed at high command. Still he was willing to fight and narrowly missed victories in the Shenandoah.

LEFT: Personal items of the great Jackson sit atop a patriotic Confederate songsheet of "Stonewall Jackson's Way." The old high-topped forage cap was not his favorite, but he wore it at times. The spurs were on his boots at his mortal wounding. The white cloth shows blood from his wound. ABOVE: The fateful bullet hole in the sleeve of Jackson's raincoat.

RIGHT: One of the most dashing and colorful of the middle level Confederate generals was the gallant John B. Gordon, who began the war as a captain and by its end rose to become a major general and the last commander of the remnant of the proud old II Corps of the Army of Northern Virginia. He became one of Lee's favorites, and in the years after the war a leading champion of peaceful reconciliation and brotherhood. He was also one of the most eloquent – if inaccurate – chroniclers of the Confederate side of the war. **FACING PAGE, TOP LEFT:** A map of the battle of Fredericksburg, Virginia, prepared by Confederate topographical engineers shortly after the action. It shows the line held by Stonewall Jackson on the right wing of the Rebel position. **FACING PAGE, TOP RIGHT:** For all of the excellent appointments made by Jefferson Davis, none was more unfortunate and unjustifiable than that of his West Point friend and classmate Leonidas Polk to the rank of lieutenant general and corps commander. There was no more incompetent officer in either army.

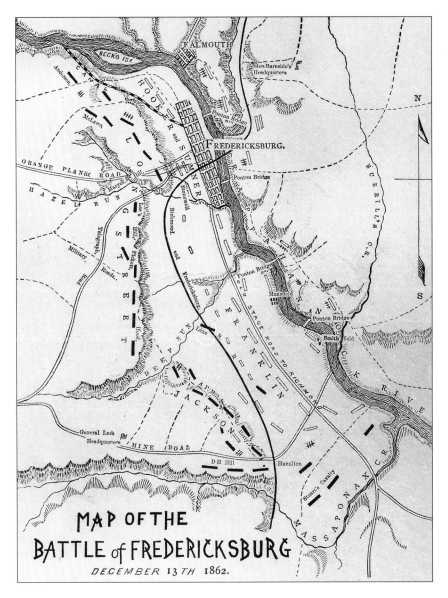

MAP OF THE
BATTLE of FREDERICKSBURG
DECEMBER 13TH 1862.

ABOVE: William J. Hardee, a leading pre-war tactical theoretician, became a corps leader known as "Old Reliable" in the Army of Tennessee.

when it was organized, and led it at Fredericksburg in December, and then at Chancellorsville the following May. There he led it and other troops on the celebrated flank march and surprise attack that routed a Federal army twice Lee's size. The success came at the cost of Jackson himself, mortally wounded accidentally by his own men.

None of Lee's other lieutenants were Jackson's equal, though A.P. Hill came close at times. Put in command of the III Corps when it was formed prior to Gettysburg, Hill gave spotty service until his death in action a week before the surrender. Still, he was far better than most of the men who held corps

command in the Confederacy's other armies, for Lee had undoubtedly the best, largely because he trained them himself. The chief lieutenants in the Army of Tennessee ranged from the utterly incompetent Leonidas Polk, appointed to command for no reason other than his boyhood friendship with Jefferson Davis, to William J. Hardee, widely respected, certainly able, but hesitant at high responsibility. A host of others came and went – D.H. Hill, Thomas C. Hindman, Simon Buckner, Breckinridge, Benjamin F. Cheatham, A.P. Stewart – all reflecting the troubled nature of that army from its very inception.

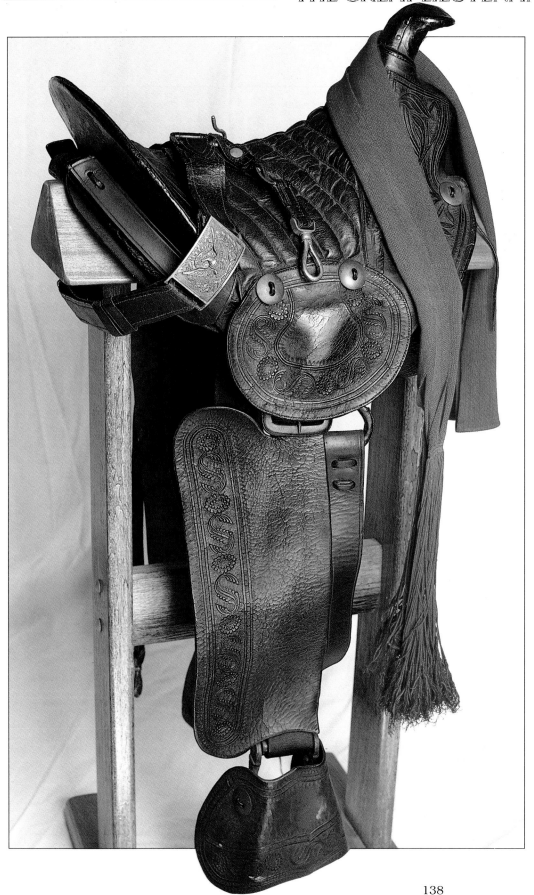

By contrast, though Union corps commanders generally did not show the concentrated brilliance of Jackson or the almost unfailing reliability of Longstreet, on the whole they were more stable and of a kind than the wildly erratic remainder of the Confederate lieutenants. Several were standouts, of course, and those who rose early, like Sherman,

McPherson, Meade and Thomas, ended the war in command of whole armies. Behind them lay a solid core of other men, perhaps only marginally less able. In the Army of the Potomac there were many, their skills unfortunately eclipsed to an extent by their being pitted against Lee and his mighty minions. No star burned brighter than that of John Reynolds, at the head of the old I Corps. Reportedly

FACING PAGE LEFT: The saddle in which Yankee Major General John F. Reynolds was sitting when he was killed at Gettysburg. He was wearing the sword belt and perhaps the sash when he fell. FACING PAGE RIGHT: Some western Confederate generals wore a distinctive pleated front uniform blouse instead of the more common variety seen almost universally elsewhere. This one belonged to Lieutenant General Simon Bolivar Buckner.

LEFT: Perhaps the Union's premier untutored battle commander was General John "Black Jack" Logan of Illinois. ABOVE: Command of the Army of the Potomac was offered to John F. Reynolds, who turned it down just days before he fell at Gettysburg.

RIGHT: This photo of part of the battlefield at Gettysburg was taken by one of Mathew Brady's assistants less than two weeks after the battle. It shows the area where General Daniel Sickles was severely wounded, losing his leg.
BELOW: Part of the battlefield toll at Antietam, where Sedgwick and other future Yankee corps commanders first showed their capacity for leadership.

he was offered command of the army in June, just before Gettysburg, but declined. Meade assumed the command instead, and Reynolds gave his life on the first day's fighting at Gettysburg, helping hold the line against desperate odds in order to buy time for the rest of his army to reach the field and win the ultimate triumph two days later.

Another man who helped save the Yankee victory did so the following day, July 2. Gouverneur K. Warren helped to hold and defend the most strategic spot on the battlefield, a hill called Little Round Top, and thereby preserved the entire Union position. For that and more services to follow, he won command of the V Corps, which he held almost to the end, until he ran foul of Sheridan the following April. Even more dashing was John Sedgwick, at the head of the VI Corps, who fought with distinction at Antietam and Fredericksburg and into the

Wilderness in 1864. Beloved of his men, he was utterly fearless: perhaps too fearless. At Spotsylvania in May 1864, staff aides warned him to keep low for fear of Rebel sharpshooters. Contemptuously, he declared that the Confederates could not hit an elephant at that range – moments before a bullet slammed into his head.

There were men just as able west of the Alleghenies, and that was where the Federals had an edge at this level of command. Among the several corps that eventually made up Sherman's army group in 1864, there were a number of men who were superior to most of the Confederate lieutenants arrayed against them. Henry Slocum would eventually rise to army command by war's end, having seen service both east and west. Oliver O. Howard commanded a corps both in the Army of the Potomac and the Army of the Cumberland, and

LEFT: Major General Gouverneur K. Warren, who as an engineer helped save Little Round Top, thereby preserving the left of Meade's line at Gettysburg. It won him a future corps command with the V Corps, which he would lose in a feud with Philip Sheridan in the last days of the war. **ABOVE:** Warren's moment of glory, as he stands atop Little Round Top, helping organize the last-minute defense that repulsed Confederate assaults.

would later command an army. Gordon Granger saved the army in the aftermath of the debacle at Chickamauga. Most notable of all was John A. Logan of Illinois. Unlike all the rest, he had no formal military training and was not a graduate of West Point. Rather, he was a prominent Democratic politician before the war, given a commission solely as a recruiting incentive for other Democrats to

enlist for the Union. Yet he steadily rose and showed both competence and combative ferocity. By mid-1864 he commanded the XV Corps, and when McPherson fell in action Logan was next in line for command of the Army of the Tennessee, though he did not get it. Late that year, when Grant was dissatisfied with the slow Thomas, he gave Logan orders to assume command of his army, but circumstances changed and Thomas retained the command. Had Logan actually assumed the position, he would have been the only non-professional of the war to lead a major army in the field.

FACING PAGE LEFT: Major General Henry Slocum, one of Sherman's western corps commanders. **FACING PAGE RIGHT:** Oliver O. Howard would rise to army command.

LEFT: The fence along the cornfield at Antietam, one of the most hotly contested pieces of ground of the entire war. At Antietam and elsewhere Major General John Sedgwick (above), distinguished himself. He would live less than two years, though, until a sharpshooter's bullet cut him down just after he boasted that enemy riflemen could not "hit an elephant at this range."

CHAPTER ELEVEN

THE EXECUTIVES

Logan was an example of an entirely different kind of general; a kind that achieved and held a largely undue prominence in this war, on both sides. They were called "political generals" and were men appointed because of their connections or their pre-war status as leading statesmen; men whose popularity could be counted on to promote enlistments or bolster the loyalty of wavering states or elements of the population.

President Abraham Lincoln, with a much larger and more diverse territory and populace, was perforce required to give more of such commissions than Davis. The largest non-native minority in the North was that of the Irish. Hence Lincoln gave

ABOVE: General Sweeney had no claim to a commission other than his influence with Irish voters.
FACING PAGE: Franz Sigel brought the support of many Germans, but proved incompetent.

generalships to Thomas F. Meagher and Thomas Sweeney. The largest non-English speaking element was that of the tens of thousands of Germans, especially in New York and Missouri. Consequently, Franz Sigel, Carl Schurz, Alexander von Schimmelfennig, and more, became generals and even corps commanders, with Sigel for a time commanding a small army. Poles were important, too, so Wladimir Krzyzanowski was made a general, though few could even pronounce his name, and many of these generals spoke such faulty English that in the heat of battle they reverted to their native tongues, making things just a bit difficult for their

subordinates. None were competent commanders, but as objects of pride for their fellow immigrants their elevation lured tens of thousands into the Union blue.

Democratic politicians loyal to the Republican war effort, like Logan, also expected their share of generalships. Bumblers such as Daniel Sickles actually rose to corps command, and Benjamin F. Butler of Massachusetts was actually one of the senior generals in the entire service, commanding the Army of the James, until Grant finally managed to weed him out of command. Almost to a man, none of these generals-by-expedience had any military training or ability, Logan and a few others excepted. Their being in the uniform at all was a necessary evil for the greater war effort, but they cost the lives of thousands by their ineptitude, leading Union chief of staff Henry W. Halleck to comment that it was "but little better than murder" to give commands to such men.

The situation was much better in the Confederacy. Davis made far fewer political appointments, and generally better ones. Only a few

ABOVE: Major General Daniel Sickles, seated, shows the price he paid for his incompetence at Gettysburg. Unseen are the hundreds of soldiers who paid for it with their lives. Many of them had been induced to enlist by Sickles and other prominent politicians. **RIGHT:** In 1862, on the Virginia Peninsula, Sickles' men stand in their line. So many of them will fall at Gettysburg that Sickles' III Corps of the Army of the Potomac will cease to exist.

politicians rose to the level of major general, most notably Howell Cobb of Georgia, John C. Breckinridge of Kentucky, and Thomas C. Hindman of Arkansas. All three of these proved to be good choices, especially the latter two. Breckinridge was one of the best division commanders in the west, and rose briefly to corps command, while Hindman did the same, and for a time commanded the Army of the Trans-Mississippi. Neither did Davis have to grant commissions to lure ethnic minorities, for the South was almost exclusively Anglo-Saxon in makeup. He appointed his share of failures, like ex-governor of Virginia Henry Wise, but for the most part, perhaps because he made fewer such appointments, the impact of Davis' commissioning inexperienced amateurs was far less detrimental.

On both sides, many of the amateur and political appointees were assigned to the kinds of commands that best suited their pre-war experience as statesmen and businessmen. For every general leading troops in the field, there was another one whose saddle was strapped to a desk. Both North and South were divided into a number of

LEFT: Politics made stranger generals than bedfellows. The Pole Wladimir Krzyzanowski was well liked, but not much of a general. TOP: Henry A. Wise of Virginia was even less of a commander, and a constant thorn in Jeff Davis' side as well. ABOVE: General Benjamin F. Butler, seated on the chair, was little better.

RIGHT: Meade's capable chief of staff A.A. Humphreys became a major general and a corps commander by the end of the war. Though never an outstanding commander, he was well liked and one of the many able administrators upon whose abilities a modern army depended.
FAR RIGHT AND FACING PAGE: The charge of Humphreys' division in the Battle of Fredericksburg in December 1862. Noted war artist Alfred R. Waud captured the scene for the Northern illustrated press.

geographical departments, districts, and even sub-districts, all of which had to be administered, both to preserve civil order and to provide materiel or manpower support to the armies in the field.

A few such departments were massive, like the Confederacy's Trans-Mississippi, which was literally a third of the nation, and while it had its own small army and a few engagements of note, it was almost wholly an administrative command, so dominated politically, civilly, and militarily by its commander

that it became known as "Kirby Smith-dom." More often the departments were simply the outline of a state or states combined, while in the Confederacy they often came down to those portions of states that were behind current Confederate lines. Occasionally a fighting general like Breckinridge or Simon Buckner commanded such a department, but usually only when it was close to Federal lines and enemy action could be expected to require a commander's combat skills. Mostly the department commanders were administrators like Cobb or Samuel Jones.

TOP: E.P. Alexander served as chief of artillery in Lee's I Corps. ABOVE: Howell Cobb was one of two professional politicians who became major generals in the Confederacy.

ABOVE: General Josiah Gorgas, capable ordnance chief of the Confederacy. TOP RIGHT: General Herman Haupt, chief of the U.S. Military Railroad, who kept Lincoln's trains running. RIGHT: William N. Pendleton, Chief of Artillery of the Army of Northern Virginia.

Then there was another sort of general: the staff officer. Most of them on both sides were of lesser ranks, usually no higher than colonel, but in a few cases such men wore stars. In Lee's army, the chiefs of artillery of the I and II Corps, E.P. Alexander and A.L. Long, became brigadiers. Lee's chief of staff Robert H. Chilton was also made a brigadier late in the war, while William W. Mackall, chief of staff in the Army of Tennessee, also became a brigadier. Lee's chief engineer, Walter H. Stevens, and his

army chief of artillery William N. Pendleton, won stars before war's end. Out in the far west, Kirby Smith's chief of staff William R. Boggs also achieved a brigadiership.

Staff officers more frequently became generals in the Union services. Grant's right-hand man, John A. Rawlins, finished the war a brigadier. Andrew A. Humphries wore a star while on Meade's staff, and Herman Haupt, Grant's chief engineer and the overseer of the United States Military Railroads, became a brigadier.

Back in the capitals, in the respective war departments, military men not infrequently rose to high rank administering their bureaus. James Hammond wore a star as surgeon general of the Union Armies. Josiah Gorgas, chief of the Ordnance Department in Richmond, became a general in the last months of the war. So did the quartermasters general on both sides, Montgomery Meigs for the North and Alexander R. Lawton for the South, and the commissary generals as well. And, of course, the adjutant generals, like Samuel Cooper and the Union's Lorenzo Thomas, got their stars, though they never set foot on a battlefield. Theirs were the largely unsung and unremembered problems of paperwork and administrative detail, yet without their thankless toils at their desks the generals out in the field would have had no men, weapons, transportation or clothing, nor anything else with which to go forward and win their glories.

ABOVE LEFT: Lorenzo Thomas, largely ineffectual adjutant and inspector general of the Union army, was sidetracked and replaced by war's end. **ABOVE:** Quartermaster General Montgomery C. Meigs kept the Union armies fed and supplied, setting the highest standards for logistical support of "modern" armies.

CHAPTER TWELVE

FRONT LINE GENERALS

ABOVE: John Jones, though not too able, was brave, and like many of the brave, died at the head of his command. **FACING PAGE:** Union General Jeff C. Davis (left) was a leader who inspired by example.

F irst to last, the glory boys were the men who led the brigades and divisions North and South. In an era when the men in the ranks expected their colonels and generals to go into battle with them, and when personal example could be all-important in maintaining esprit, these generals had almost no choice but to place themselves at the forefront of their men to lead them into action. For many it was never a matter of choice. Their own enthusiasm and fighting instincts demanded that they be where the contest was hottest.

Such men emerged early in the war, mostly as regimental colonels. Gordon was one, a man with no military experience or training, who proved to be one of the boldest and most effective combat leaders of the war. Leading his Georgia regiment through the fights in 1862, he strode onto the field at Antietam in September hardly suspecting that every Yankee bullet on the field seemed aimed at him. He was hit once, but stayed with his command. A second and a third time he felt the enemy lead, yet still remained with his men. A fourth bullet delivered yet another painful wound, and a fifth narrowly missed killing him, passing through the crown of his hat. Finally, a sixth missile hit him full in the face while he still stood on the line with his men. Toppling over

FACING PAGE: The banner of the U.S. 7th Kentucky Infantry lists the battles in which it participated. In many – if not most – of them, the Kentuckians would have followed their brigade general into action. Such frontline commanders took great personal risks in order to inspire their men to go into the fight and risk their own lives. **LEFT:** The battleflag of the 6th Kentucky Infantry, C.S.A. At its head Generals Roger Hanson and Benjamin H. Helm met their deaths. **BELOW:** Yankees, too, followed their generals into battle. Here the 3d Rhode Island goes into action in South Carolina in 1862.

unconscious, his face buried in his hat, he bled profusely and would probably have drowned in his own blood but for the fortuitous hole made by that earlier bullet. It drained the hat, and Gordon miraculously lived to fight again, and again.

A fighting Irishman from Arkansas, Patrick R. Cleburne, achieved a reputation as the "Stonewall of the West" at the head of his division in the Army of Tennessee. From Shiloh to Perryville in 1862 he made a reputation as a solid fighter, then won renewed laurels at Stones River. And at Chickamauga, on the second day, it was his division and Breckinridge's that delivered such brutal attacks on the Federal left that Rosecrans weakened his center just at the point, and at the moment, that a massive Rebel attack swept forward. Cleburne was always to be found in the midst of his men, cheering and inspiring them, as when he covered

the retreat after the debacle at Missionary Ridge. Indeed, it was his concept of the need to expose himself thus that finally brought his end at Franklin, Tennessee, in late 1864, when he and five other Confederate generals perished.

Some, like Lewis A. Armistead, seemed virtually to court death. At Gettysburg, during the great assault on July 3, known erroneously as Pickett's Charge, Armistead placed himself on foot in front of his Virginia brigade, put his hat on the tip of his sword, and led his men over a stone wall into the face of thousands of Yankee rifles. He never recrossed that wall. Other generals paid the same price trying to steady their men in the face of retreat. On May 5, 1864, during the Battle of the Wilderness, Brigadier General John M. Jones saw his brigade waver, then fall back in the face of a vicious Yankee onslaught. Trying to rally his men by a display of calm and courage, he sat on his horse in the middle of a road "gazing at the approaching enemy" as if completely unmindful of the danger. He looked too long, and one of them brought him down with a fatal ball.

There was just as much heroism – or foolhardiness – on the Federal side of the line, and

ABOVE: Another view of the Battle of Shiloh. While popular prints like this always showed generals on horseback, sword in the air, in heroic pose, in fact this did not vary widely from the behavior of many battle commanders. **LEFT:** A sketch showing preparation of defensive works on the Brock Road in the Battle of the Wilderness in May 1864. A good general paid as much attention to his men's protection as to leading them into action.

there, too, the armies suffered from the fact that the best battlefield leaders were often among the first to fall, thanks to their necessary personal exposure. Most, however, managed to come through the war, battered perhaps, but alive. Pennsylvania's John W. Geary compiled an enviable record on both sides of the mountains at the head of his division of the XII Corps, and at the Battle of Lookout Mountain in November 1863 achieved a bit of immortality in the misnamed "Battle Above the Clouds."

Over in the XX Corps there fought another colorful division commander, notable for his name if nothing else. Major General Jefferson C. Davis took a lot of teasing for the similarity between his own name and that of his enemies' president. But

LEFT: When General John Jones faced his horse toward the Federal foe in the Battle of the Wilderness, his foot was in the stirrup when the fatal ball brought him down. He preferred death to the dishonor of his brigade fleeing in the face of the enemy. **BELOW:** Part of the area known as the Wilderness, which claimed the lives of several generals on both sides.

no one teased him on the battlefield. When his division along with others was put to rout at Chickamauga, Davis was the only one to rally his men, end the panic, and turn them back to the battlefield where the rest of the army desperately held out. More daring was Israel B. Richardson, whose nickname "Fighting Dick" said all that needed saying. He promised repeatedly that he would ask

ABOVE: Jeff C. Davis, one of the battle-hardened leaders at Chattanooga and other western battlefields. **ABOVE RIGHT:** The summit of Lookout Mountain at right and, in the distance, Chattanooga and the Tennessee River. **RIGHT:** A bird's-eye view of Chattanooga, where men like Sheridan, Hooker, Thomas, and other generals, inspired the Federals to victory. **FACING PAGE:** Yankee General Israel B. Richardson, a front-line leader killed at Antietam.

no man to go where he would not go himself, and he never did. At Antietam he was in the thick of the fight, sensing victory over Lee if only the Federals would push a little harder at Bloody Lane. While trying to make that push himself an exploding artillery shell added his name to the roster of 3,000 other casualties suffered in that bitter battle-within-a-battle.

Perhaps none of them equalled the magnificent Winfield Scott Hancock. At Antietam he commanded a brigade in the old VI Corps, then assumed command of Richardson's division after his

FAR LEFT: A romantic print of a scene from the Battle of Antietam. Here future great generals like Winfield Scott Hancock, John B. Gordon, George Meade, Joseph Hooker, and more, showed their capacity both for command and also for inspiring men to follow them into the inferno of action.

LEFT: Winfield Scott Hancock, shown in his uniform as major general and commander of the II Corps of the Army of the Potomac.

wounding. On every field Hancock distinguished himself, but nowhere more than at Gettysburg. There, on the first day, as the Federal lines were disintegrating and the position on Cemetery Hill was in danger of giving way, Hancock arrived just in time to take command until Meade could arrive. By his very presence, inspiring beyond description, he put heart into his men and steel into their lines. When the commander of the III Corps fell on July 2, Hancock assumed its command. Then, on July 3, with the approach of the massive Confederate assault, it was Hancock who stood in the lines directing the defense that shattered the attack, taking a bad wound himself in the process and nearly losing his life.

CHAPTER THIRTEEN

THE GREAT CAVALRYMEN

ABOVE: Grant's protege, James H. Wilson rose to become one of the Union's leading cavalry generals. In the end he commanded a virtual army of horsemen sweeping across the South.

Even the boldest of the bold, like Hancock, were eclipsed in the public mind, and in the memory of posterity, by a special few who so captured the imagination of the era and posterity that their fame often exceeds the real worth of their exploits. Nothing so appealed to the romantic mind then and later as a man on a horse. The very thought conjured images of cavaliers bedecked in plumes, atop fire-breathing steeds. It is no wonder that the cavalry in both armies during the Civil War, especially in the romance-ridden Confederate service, was self-consciously flamboyant. No wonder that the generals who led that mounted arm, North and South, quickly earned a special place in their

peoples' hearts.

Of them all, none would exceed in romance and dash the incomparable cavalier in gray, James Ewell Brown "Jeb" Stuart. He began the war as colonel of the 1st Virginia Cavalry, but even that took a romantic turn when some dubbed his outfit the "Black Horse Cavalry," giving it a sinister, almost brigandish flavor. He showed an early aptitude for the classic task of the mounted arm – reconnaissance, raiding, protecting an army's flanks – but revealed as well a theatrical bent that at times lessened his effectiveness. Performing for Lee, he made one brilliant raid after another, riding around the Yankee army, disrupting communications,

destroying supplies, and gathering valuable intelligence. Quite rightfully Lee thought of Stuart as the "eyes" of his army. But Stuart could not resist the temptation also to plunder, to bring his captures back with him, and to take unnecessary risks for the sake of the adventure, even when they impeded the performance of his actual task. Indeed, during the Gettysburg Campaign Stuart was not where Lee expected him to be, but was off on another raid, thus denying to Lee the intelligence that he desperately needed as he operated in the enemy's country. Still, by the time of his untimely death from a mortal wound in the Battle of Yellow Tavern, on May 11, 1864, Stuart was universally regarded as without a peer in the East, blue or gray.

Stuart's replacement was a different sort entirely. Wade Hampton was a South Carolinian, too genteel to affect the gaudy plumage and flamboyant garb of Stuart. But that did not mean he did not answer the same impulses of gallantry and daring. At Gettysburg he found himself isolated from his command and facing a Yankee cavalryman at some distance. While the soldier fired his Spencer repeating carbine, Hampton sat his saddle and returned fire with his pistol. Then, when the Federal's weapon jammed, Hampton held his own fire until the jam was cleared, whereupon the two resumed firing, both taking wounds. A year later, now in command of the cavalry corps of the Army of Northern Virginia, Hampton planned the daring "Beefsteak Raid," in which a herd of 3,000 beeves was captured behind Yankee lines and driven halfway around the Federal army besieging Petersburg, to reach the hungry mouths of Lee's army.

ABOVE: The popular image of a cavalry charge is depicted in this print of a Union horse assault at Cold Harbor, Virginia, in 1862. Even more than in the infantry, the cavalry generals led from the saddle.

The Federals, too, had their dashing cavaliers. When Phil Sheridan led a small army in the Shenandoah in 1864, he seemed to have a constellation of colorful horse generals under him: A.T.A. Torbert, Thomas Davies, David McM. Gregg, and, most notorious of all, George A. Custer, a man with a positive instinct for battle, and a single-minded determination to throw himself and his men into the thickest of a fight and trust to "Custer's luck" to see them through. Vain, egotistical, prone to the role of martinet, still Custer was one of the ablest subordinate cavalrymen of the war.

But others achieved greater things, if not greater glory. Benjamin Grierson conducted probably the

LEFT: The premier cavalryman of the Confederacy, J.E.B. Stuart rose from command of a Virginia regiment to a lieutenant generalcy and command of the cavalry corps at the Army of Northern Virginia. **ABOVE:** A romantic depiction of a Confederate cavalryman. In fact, the average Rebel horseman was far less well equipped. **FACING PAGE:** Some of the military effects of J.E.B. Stuart, including his saddle, plumed hat, saber, sword belt, and gauntlets.

FACING PAGE: After Stuart's death, General Wade Hampton of South Carolina took command of Lee's cavalry. The giant Hampton was oft-wounded in action, and just as combative as Stuart. ABOVE: A view from a "crow's nest" observation tower behind Union lines looking toward Confederate lines at Petersburg in the distance. RIGHT: The premier cavalry generals in Grant's command. They are, left to right, Wesley Merritt, David McM. Gregg, Philip H. Sheridan, Thomas A. Davies, James H. Wilson, and A.T.A. Torbert.

most brilliant raid of the war in 1863, when he led barely more than 1,500 men on a back-breaking march south through the entire length of Mississippi in the rear of Confederate lines. It was a diversion to help allow Grant to make his successful envelopment of the Rebel position at Vicksburg, and in the process it destroyed railroads, telegraph lines, tons of Rebel war materiel, and thoroughly disrupted Confederate operations in the entire region. More devastating still was the raid led by

ABOVE: The charge of the 6th U.S. Cavalry on Stuart's command during the Peninsula Campaign on May 9, 1862. In fact, the flashing sabers were seldom used, the soldiers more often employing them as meat spits, and the generals wearing them for show and ceremony.

General James H. Wilson, once a lowly staff officer with Grant, who in 1865 led a small army of cavalry through Alabama in a lightning raid almost unparalleled for destruction by any similar exploit of the war.

It was also Wilson, in the end, who was the only Yankee cavalryman to substantially best the undoubted master horseman of the entire war, Nathan Bedford Forrest. Literally an untutored genius of war – he was marginally literate, though extremely intelligent – Forrest began the war a private in the 7th Tennessee Cavalry. By 1865 he was a lieutenant general commanding a small army of cavalry, and behind him lay a series of the most stunning defeats ever suffered by Yankee horsemen during the war. Time after time he appeared where it seemed he could not possibly be, defeated numbers considerably superior to his own, then reappeared somewhere else to wreak more havoc. "That devil Forrest," he was called by his foes, and in 1864 Sherman detached inordinate men and means to try to stop – unsuccessfully – his depredations on

FAR LEFT: An example of the penchant of some cavalry generals for show and resplendance. Federal General A.T.A. Torbert displays glorious facial whiskers.
LEFT: Perhaps the most gifted natural combat leader of all horsemen, Nathan Bedford Forrest rose from obscurity to become the most feared of Rebel mounted leaders.

Union supply and communications. Frighteningly fearless himself, Forrest personally killed more of his foes than any other general on either side, and even killed one of his own officers in a fight – after the officer had already shot him in the abdomen. There was no dash, no dress parade finery about Forrest and his command; just cold, calculated, ruthless daring and efficiency. Opinions will always vary, but many would argue that he was, taken all in all, the greatest cavalryman who ever lived.

Thus they are remembered as the greatest, the boldest, the most colorful, and so on. The generals blue and gray have never released their grip on the human imagination, and probably never will. Whether patriots or poltroons, courageous or cowardly, they were what the public saw and most identified with then and later, often to the exclusion of the men in the ranks who bore the brunt of the battle. Yet it has always been so, a phenomenon that detracts not at all from the fact that these few special men deserve to be remembered.

ABOVE: A silver cup belonging to Nathan Bedford Forrest. Such trappings were out of the ordinary for a man more given to drinking from a rude canteen.

THE BATTLES

ABOVE: The 73d Ohio Infantry marching off to war from Chillicothe in 1862, a scene repeated all across the country, North and South, as American youth sought adventure.

THE BATTLES

There were more than 10,000 fights, from the greatest of battles, like Gettysburg, to the completely forgotten little skirmishes at places such as Jones' Hay Station, Arkansas. Few can agree on what constitutes exactly the first engagement. Shots were fired in obscure places even before the guns first opened in earnest at Fort Sumter; opinions divide on just when and where the last shots were fired, as well, especially since the Confederate commerce raider CSS *Shenandoah* continued to capture Yankee merchant vessels for almost six months after the Rebel armies surrendered.

But no one disputes that of all the elements that made up the American Civil War – political, social, economic, and more – it was the battles that most captured the attention and imagination of the people North and South, then and now. It was the ultimate test, the arena where history's decisions came down to epic clashes between the mightiest armies ever seen on the continent, and to the intensely personal micro-battles of one man against another. More than this, there was an incredible variety in them, from attacks on massive stationary fortresses, to open field battles, to sieges, and even epic duels between ironclad warships on the waters. Every one was different. In every one, the blood, determination, and heroism were the same.

LEFT: A romantic lithograph depicting sword-wielding General Phil Sheridan leading his men into battle at Cedar Creek, in 1864. It was the kind of idealized picture of war that was soon belied by the real horrors.

CHAPTER FOURTEEN

FORT SUMTER

In the decades following the winning of its independence, the United States commenced construction of a chain of large masonry forts guarding each of the harbors and river mouths along its Atlantic and Gulf coastlines. Each was designed to defend against attack from seaward; no one conceived that they might, instead, be attacked from the land, from the rear, and by fellow Americans. Many of these forts were situated in Southern states, and when secession led first South Carolina, and then the other states, to pass ordinances of secession in 1860-61, these forts and their Federal garrisons immediately became bones of contention.

Confederates claimed the forts as rightfully their own, and wanted the Yankee soldiers withdrawn immediately. Several, barely manned at all, yielded without a fight. But there was one that would not.

Fort Sumter sat on an artificial island of rubble in the middle of Charleston harbor, staring in the face the South Carolina city that had always been the seedbed of secession sentiment, and where the first secession ordinance was passed in December 1860. The fort was largely unfinished as yet, with many of its guns not yet mounted on their parapets, the barracks incomplete, and some of the brick casemates still lacking their hardware and fittings.

FACING PAGE: Major Robert Anderson was truly a man caught in the middle, between his Southern sympathies, and his firm duty to his uniform. No one felt the tragedy of Fort Sumter more than he. LEFT: Others were delighted at the coming of war, none more so than the vitriolic old secessionist Edmund Ruffin, emblematic of the kind of fanaticism on both sides that brought on the war.

ABOVE: Opportunists like Louis T. Wigfall of Texas, mixed conflicting and often ill-defined personal motives into their support for secession, and war. They all lived to regret the curse they brought on the land.

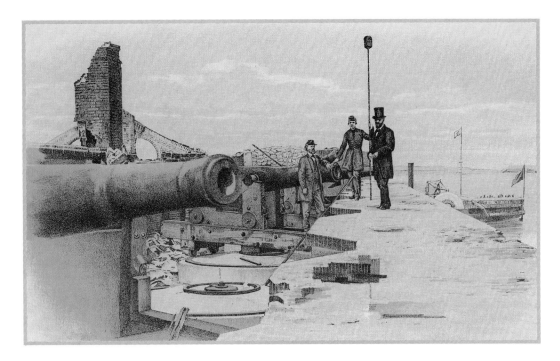

When South Carolina seceded, the fort was not yet manned, the Federal garrison in Charleston occupying Fort Moultrie and other works on the mainland. Major Robert Anderson, a Kentuckian and a slave-holder, commanded the tiny garrison of just 87 officers and men, including musicians, and as demands for turning over the fort increased in late December after the secession declaration, he feared for his exposed position in Moultrie. While negotiations fumbled on between South Carolina and Washington, he took action on his own.

On the night of Christmas, 1860, Anderson spiked the guns at Moultrie and secretly rowed his small command out to Fort Sumter. There, at least, he would not be susceptible to assault by the Confederate militia even then gathering around Charleston. His act outraged the South Carolinians, who accused him of committing a hostile act, and now there were renewed demands for the surrender

ABOVE: Within only two days of the fall of Fort Sumter, gloating Confederates were bringing cameras into the ruins to capture the scene of the fort and its conquerors. Here on the terre plain and parapet of the eastern face of the fort can be seen evidence of some of the damage done, along with two of the cannon that Anderson managed to use sporadically to return fire.

RIGHT: A youthful South Carolinian poses calmly inside the dreaded "Ironclad Battery" that had done quite a bit to wreak some of that destruction on Fort Sumter. It was from this interior that the famed old secessionist Edmund Ruffin had fired one of the first shots of the war. As irony would have it Ruffin would also fire one of the last, a bullet into his own brain in 1865, when he could not face the fact of Southern defeat. It was such extremism on both sides that had brought on the war.

of Sumter. Instead, Anderson feverishly worked to make a few of its cannon operational and get its defenses in order. For the next three-and-a-half months Anderson held out, and the Confederates held their fire. Washington tried in January to send a relief expedition by sea, but the Southerners scared the ships away. In April another supply fleet was sent, due to arrive on the twelfth.

The Confederates knew it was coming. Colonel P.G.T. Beauregard had been sent to take command in Charleston, and, with orders from the new Confederate government not to allow Sumter to be resupplied, he sent officers of his staff out to see Anderson on the afternoon of April 11. They issued another demand for surrender. Anderson refused, but hinted that he might be starved out in a few

ABOVE: As soon as the news of Sumter's fall spread, fanciful depictions of the bombardment erupted from presses around the divided nation. Few were accurate, but almost all made it look glorious – and clean.

ABOVE: More of the victors, some in civilian attire, cluster outside the sally port of the fallen fortress. It quickly became the most popular tourist spot in the South.

RIGHT: Dignitaries including governors and future generals like Wade Hampton, in the tall hat at center, inspected the fort's ruins and pronounced the achievement of its taking wonderful.

FACING PAGE: Certainly the damage done was something new in their experience, for such cannon as those used had never been fired in anger before on the continent. But Sumter would be ruined far more than this before war's end.

days anyhow without relief. Beauregard sent back another mission just after midnight, inquiring exactly when Anderson would have to leave or starve. The major said he would leave by noon on April 15 "should I not receive ... additional supplies." Knowing that the relief ships could arrive at any hour, Beauregard decided this was not good enough.

At 4:30 a.m. on April 12, 1861, the boom of a cannon echoed across the harbor, and Anderson and his men saw a sputtering shell arch high into the heavens, exploding almost directly over them. It was the signal shell to open the bombardment, and within seconds almost fifty cannon and mortars belched forth a hail of iron that, once commenced, went on continuously for the next thirty-three hours. In that time, some 3,341 cannon balls and shells would be fired at the fort, from batteries that ringed the harbor and surrounded the beleaguered Federals.

ABOVE: Charleston photographer George S. Cook took his camera into Sumter months before the bombardment to take portraits of Major Anderson and his officers. The major's calm visage belies the turmoil he was enduring inside. With typical wit for the time, Cook published his photos with the pun "Major Anderson Taken."

ABOVE: Confederate artist Conrad Wise Chapman's excellent 1863 painting of the interior of one of the gun tiers of Fort Sumter shows it much as it would have looked in 1861, the only difference being that no such tranquil scene of a gunner asleep beside his piece would have been likely. The din inside the casemates was terrible, the atmosphere choking from the acrid gunsmoke. When these mighty columbiads fired they created a concussion like an earthquake. No one slept during the day on April 12-14, 1861.

In response, Anderson had only twenty-one guns on the fort's lower casemate tier, most of them 32-pounder smoothbores. When the first Confederate shots began to strike the fort, he held his own fire. After all, there was little damage that he could do, and he hesitated to shoot back. No war had actually been declared, but making a real battle of this might lead to it. And he would not uselessly expose his men.

Morning came and went. The garrison ate their meager breakfast of fat pork and water. Only after several hours under bombardment did he form the men on the parade and give them orders. They would work a limited number of the guns in the protected casemates. There was little they could do other than maintain their honor by refusing meekly to sit idle and take a pounding.

The first Yankee shot was fired by Major Abner Doubleday, a man often erroneously credited with inventing the game of baseball. When the Confederates heard the report of his 32-pounder, they actually cheered, as they would do so from time to time for the rest of the day. They cheered in admiration of the plucky Yankees fighting back, and they cheered that their inevitable victory would not be cheapened by being unresisted.

As the hours of bombardment dragged on, the Rebels' fire became increasingly accurate, and their shot started to turn the interior of the fort into rubble. Meanwhile, the answering fire from the fort did almost no damage at all, so well were the Confederate batteries protected. After midday the wooden barracks inside Sumter caught fire, and soon burned out of control. Flying masonry also

wounded four of Anderson's soldiers. By noon Anderson also found that his supply of powder bags for charging the guns was running low, and he had to reduce firing to just six guns. Even those he silenced at nightfall. The only good news that evening was a downpour that put out the fire in the barracks. But that hardly made up for the sight of the relief fleet, which had come in sight outside the harbor that afternoon, but which declined to risk

ABOVE: Abner Doubleday happily fired the first return shot, stirred to a vengeful mood by the destruction taking place inside and outside the walls of Fort Sumter. TOP LEFT: The shattered soldiers' quarters by the parade. BOTTOM LEFT: The sally port.

the fire of Confederate guns by coming to the fort's assistance. Anderson and his men were on their own.

Rebel shells came every fifteen minutes through the night, to keep the garrison awake. The bombardment resumed in full at dawn, but Anderson could now fire only one gun every five minutes in response. The barracks took fire again, dangerously close to the powder magazine. Sumter filled with smoke and flames, and the Yankees faced the possibility of roasting or suffocation. Once again the Confederates cheered their foemen's bravery in continuing to resist. Then a shot brought down Sumter's flag, and Confederates thought that Anderson might be surrendering. Emissaries rowed out to the fort, and even though Anderson had not

intended to yield, negotiations resulted in his agreeing to evacuate the following day. At 1:30 p.m. on April 14, the bombardment stopped.

The next day, at 2:0 p.m., Major Anderson officially turned over the fort, only after firing an intended hundred-gun salute to his flag as he took it down. Tragically, an accident during the firing led to the death of a private, and cut short the salute at fifty. Two hours later, after burying Private Daniel Hough, the first man killed in the Civil War, Anderson marched out of the fort and put his men aboard transports for the trip North. As he left, he carried under his arm his beloved flag. Four years later to the day, with the war all but over, Anderson would come back to Fort Sumter and raise that same flag once more.

FACING PAGE: The officers' quarters are equally as ruined as the enlisted men's, and on the parade in front the remains of the flagstaff pays tribute to the fire directed against it. **ABOVE:** Young Confederates form a rough line on the parade, many of them recent arrivals judging from the knapsacks and blanket rolls on their backs. There is a long war ahead of them.

CHAPTER FIFTEEN

HAMPTON ROADS

ollowing Sumter's fall, North and South mobilized for battle, more states seceded to join the Confederacy, and America went to war. The first real land battle came in July, at Bull Run in Virginia, with more fights out in Missouri that fall. President Lincoln imposed a blockade of Southern ports to prevent assistance reaching the Rebels from abroad, and early in 1862 movements began to retake the Mississippi Valley from the Confederates. Federal troops were also poised to march on the new enemy capital at Richmond, Virginia, moving from a base at Fort Monroe, beside Hampton Roads, a fort that managed to remain in Yankee hands. Such a thrust from below and east

Symbols of the hopeful
Confederate Navy.
TOP: The ironclad CSS *Virginia* in a
fanciful artist's rendition.
ABOVE: The Navy Department seal.

of Richmond might be deadly effective, but it depended upon troops and supplies being brought to Fort Monroe by water from the North, and if the Rebels could break the blockade and deny access to Hampton Roads, such a thrust could be thwarted.

Almost from the first, in April 1861, when Lincoln declared the blockade, Confederates turned their minds to ways of breaking it. If Rebel ships could get through or, better yet, if Federal ships could be driven off or destroyed, then European shipping could reach Southern ports and major powers might declare the blockade ineffective, and therefore illegal.

But, as with everything else, the South had too

few warships, really only those captured at the outset when shipyards on its coastline were seized. Worse, facilities for building new vessels were almost nonexistent. The best Confederate hope was in converting vessels to its purpose, and here the new nation encountered a stroke of good fortune.

When Virginia seceded, Confederates quickly overran Federal installations in the Old Dominion. They took the Navy Yard at Norfolk and Portsmouth, and even though the evacuating Yankees attempted to destroy everything left behind, they were too hasty at their work. Machinery was still usable. Better yet, ships set afire were not entirely destroyed, especially the huge steam frigate USS *Merrimack*. She burned only to the deck line, then was scuttled. Feverishly the Confederates raised her, refitted her machinery, and then began constructing the war's first ironclad. They fitted a massive iron ram to her prow below the waterline, mounted ten heavy naval cannon on her deck, and erected a long, sloping casemate over the guns, covering it with several inches of laminated iron sheathing.

ABOVE: The *Virginia* did not ride with her deck awash as suggested here, but she was rakishly low in the water, and her real danger lay in the iron ram on her prow, just beneath the waterline. In this colorful, though largely inaccurate, print she drives that ram into the hold of the USS *Cumberland*.

TOP: Fort Monroe played silent witness to the dramatic events of March 8-9. ABOVE: Catesby Jones assumed command of the *Virginia* when Buchanan was wounded. RIGHT: Buchanan's brother J. McKean Buchanan was a lieutenant commander in the Yankee fleet that he attacked. Happily, both survived such sibling rivalry.

The plan was simple. Such a vessel, able to withstand anything the enemy could shoot at it, would steam out into the blockading fleet in Hampton Roads and either ram and sink Yankee wooden warships, or else blast them with her guns from the impervious security of the ironclad casemate. They called her the CSS *Virginia*. She was ready by March 8, 1862.

Early that morning Commodore Franklin Buchanan and his executive officer Lieutenant Catesby Jones got steam up in the *Virginia* and set out into Hampton Roads. Awaiting them was the Union fleet, chiefly the sloop *Cumberland* and the frigates *Congress* and *Minnesota*. The lumbering *Virginia* looked to the waiting Federals like "the roof of a barn belching forth smoke" as she approached, but they did not scoff for long. Her blazing guns almost destroyed the fleet. By the end of the day the *Minnesota* had run aground attempting to get away from her, the *Cumberland* had gone to the bottom, and the *Congress* was a blazing hulk. The Confederate ironclad had suffered

only the loss of her prow, and a painful leg wound for Buchanan. The next day she expected to go out and finish the *Minnesota* and any other Yankee ships in her path.

On the morning of March 9, as the *Virginia* steamed into Hampton Roads once more, her men saw in the distance a new ship that had arrived during the night. She looked like a "cheese box on a raft," thought one. She was the USS *Monitor*. The Confederates had not been the only ironclad

builders. When word of the terrible new vessel being constructed at Portsmouth reached Washington, Union naval leaders immediately commenced work on several ironclad designs of their own, in order to counter the *Virginia*. Swedish inventor John Ericsson submitted a design that called for a sleek, low hull, gliding barely above the water, with nothing projecting from it but a pilot house, smoke stacks, and a huge iron turret protecting two 11-inch smoothbore cannon, each of which could fire a solid

ABOVE: The mighty USS *Minnesota* very nearly became a casualty of the *Virginia's* blazing guns when she ran aground in Hampton Roads. Only the end of the day saved her from receiving the full attention of the Rebel monster, which steamed into the Roads again the next day expecting to have an easy time of finishing her off.

shot weighing 168 pounds. After each firing, the turret could be revolved away from the enemy to allow reloading of the guns in safety. In one of history's closest bits of timing, she was ready just as the *Virginia* was being completed, and hurried to Hampton Roads just in time.

Naval observers North and South watched anxiously to see the meeting of the two iron leviathans. At about eight a.m. the moment came. Deciding to ignore the little *Monitor*, the *Virginia* made for the helpless *Minnesota*. But then the Yankee ironclad steamed out to place herself in the way, and quickly the contest became one of iron against iron. For maneuverability, the *Monitor* had the best of it from the first. She was lighter, faster, and more agile, while the lumbering Confederate behemoth seemingly took forever to turn, and could only bring her guns to bear when turned in just the proper position, while the foe's revolving turret, though only placing two guns in opposition to ten, could fire from almost any position.

RIGHT: Midshipman Henry H. Marmaduke.
LEFT: A popular 19th century painting of the epic duel between *Monitor* and *Virginia*. Despite a few minor inaccuracies, it well depicts what the scene must have looked like – smoke, fire, and noise. **ABOVE**: By contrast, this summer 1862 scene on the deck of the *Monitor* could not appear more peaceful, as the crew sit for midday meal and a smoke.

For the next two hours they gave each other undivided attention. The two vessels steamed round and round each other, firing almost constantly. The *Virginia* got marginally the worst of it from the beginning, the enemy's shells cracking and knocking loose several of the iron plates protecting the

TOP: Unfortunately, no overall photograph exists that shows the entire *Monitor*. This picture was taken in the summer of 1862, showing the turret as it still evidences the effects of some of the *Virginia's* shot. The sloping roof of the new pilothouse appears in the distance.

FAR RIGHT: Lieutenant John Worden was commanding his first ship when he took over the *Monitor*, and the March 9 engagement was the only one in which he would do so, being wounded late in the day while in his pilothouse.

RIGHT: Midshipman Hardin B. Littlepage was one of those on the *Virginia* firing guns at Worden. Most of them were young, and very brave.

casemate. Had Lieutenant John Worden been able to concentrate his fire against a particular point on the Rebel ironclad, he might have broken through. If so, then one exploding shell inside the casemate would most likely have put the *Virginia* out of action.

Meanwhile, aboard the *Monitor* there were problems, too. The machinery controlling the revolving turret was clumsy and hard to operate. Finally the gunners just let the turret keep turning, and fired their guns "on the fly" as the enemy turned into view through the gun ports. The Confederate shells did the turret no real harm,

causing only dents, but occasionally an impact knocked loose a bolt head inside the turret, turning it into a deadly missile that shot across the interior.

The *Virginia* tried to ram the *Monitor*, not knowing yet of the missing ram, but moved so slowly that the ships only glanced off each other harmlessly. Finally the *Monitor* pulled away when a chance shot struck the pilot house and blinded Worden. His executive Lieutenant, Samuel D. Greene, took command, but when he turned back to resume the contest, he saw the *Virginia* steaming back to Portsmouth. Each vessel thought the other had given up.

The battle itself was inconclusive, though the blockade remained in effect and the *Virginia* never again did battle with Union ships. Two months later her own crew destroyed her when Norfolk was recaptured by the Federals. The *Monitor* fought again on the James River, but ineffectively, and finally sank in a storm that December off North Carolina. But they had started something, these vessels. "Ironclad fever" swept North and South, and scores of new monsters were laid down, inaugurating the modern era of naval warfare, and putting an end forever to the days of iron men in wooden ships.

ABOVE: In the summer of 1862, the officers of the *Monitor* sat for a cameraman, posing before the turret that had shielded them and their guns in the epic battle. Lieutenant Samuel D. Greene, who assumed command after Worden's wounding, sits on the chair at left. Some of the others are new transfers who did not participate in the battle.

CHAPTER SIXTEEN

SECOND MANASSAS

T he Union lost its bid to take Richmond in the spring of 1862. Despite stopping the *Virginia*, Union operations on the Peninsula below Richmond stalled. Worse, General Thomas J. "Stonewall" Jackson's Confederates defeated three separate armies in Virginia's Shenandoah Valley. Washington itself began to fear that Rebel soldiers would be seen at its gates, and President Lincoln hastily called a new commander to assemble a new army from the fragments left and protect the Capital.

He summoned General John Pope, a flamboyant, egotistical officer who had enjoyed some limited success on the Mississippi. He was to put together

ABOVE: Major General John Pope was cursed by his own ego, McClellan's petulance, and Robert E. Lee. **FACING PAGE:** Here on the crest of Henry Hill at Second Manassas they all defeated him.

the new Army of Virginia, and with it march south to threaten Lee's rear while he faced the Army of the Potomac under George B. McClellan, still on the Peninsula.

Multiple misfortunes ensued. Pope offended almost everyone, especially his own officers and men, by his conceit and boastfulness. Then Lee soundly defeated McClellan on the Peninsula, but the Army of the Potomac did not leave, only settling down for the summer, while a petulant McClellan did nothing to hold Lee in place, and also refused to send any of his own men to reinforce Pope. Still, Pope would have three corps, totaling 38,000 men, commanded by Generals Franz Sigel, Nathaniel

RIGHT: The man who gave Union commanders headaches, General Robert E. Lee conducted his first offensive at Second Manassas. ABOVE: A March 1862 photograph of the earthwork defenses erected around Manassas Junction, some of them put up by the Confederates, and then used by the occupying Federals until Jackson came to call. FACING PAGE: More fortifications left by the Rebels, and adapted by the Yankees, here men of the 13th Massachusetts. All too soon they would be fighting not for Manassas, but for their lives. TOP LEFT (inset): The house used as headquarters by Generals Pope and McDowell near Cedar Mountain. TOP CENTER (inset): A few of the casualties of Cedar Mountain.
TOP RIGHT (inset): More of Manassas before Jackson.

Banks, and Irvin McDowell – all three just a step above incompetents.

Against them would be the great Lee, fresh from his victories against McClellan. Almost disdainfully he divided his army in Richmond, right in the face of McClellan. He sent Jackson with 24,000 to central Virginia when Pope's new army advanced to the Rappahannock River, and soon afterward received the great news that Jackson had struck again, catching Banks and 8,000 Yankees isolated from the rest of their army and taking them by surprise. The Battle of Cedar Mountain, on August 9, was a Federal disaster. Worse, despite orders to leave the

Peninsula and join with Pope, McClellan did not start to move at last until August 13. Meanwhile, Pope could do nothing but stay where he was in central Virginia, between Lee and Washington, and wait for McClellan to arrive. McClellan would never arrive. Lee would get to Pope first. By mid-August, the Federal Army of Virginia numbered more than 75,000, thanks to additional reinforcements, but Lee had some 55,000 on their way to rendezvous against them. Being outnumbered never frightened

LEFT: Stonewall Jackson's lightning raid on Manassas Junction, Pope's chief supply base, struck a devastating blow to the Federals. Scenes like this one of a ruined locomotive were spread all across the Manassas plain in Jackson's wake. Cut the railroads, and you cut the flow of food, men, and weapons.

Lee. Instead, he thought only of the offensive, and now he planned a bold move to send Jackson and 24,000 men on a wide move around Pope to hit his rear, while General James Longstreet, commanding the balance of the Army of Northern Virginia, would occupy Pope's attention in his front.

Jackson struck with devastating effectiveness. He moved around Pope's flank and arrived at Manassas Junction, an important rail center near the site of the war's first battle just over a year before. Manassas was Pope's supply base, and Jackson hit and destroyed it completely. Pope had no choice but to pull back from the Rappahannock to Manassas, in order to reestablish his

ABOVE: Nothing was so calculated to crush the spirit and optimism of the men in an army as the sight of their supply base in ruins, their stockpiles of stores and ammunition destroyed, and their link with succor and safety broken. Destroy a supply base, and half the job of defeating an army was accomplished, as Jackson and Lee knew better than any others.

A dozen Federals lounge in the summer heat near Blackburn's Ford, on Bull Run, on July 4, 1862. It is a national holiday for them, but in a few weeks they would fight for their lives on these fields.

ABOVE: One of the most unsatisfactory generals of the entire war was the German Franz Sigel. Influential, egotistical, and utterly incompetent, he also lacked courage on more than one occasion. At Second Manassas he added no luster to his reputation.

communications with Washington. Meanwhile, Jackson's job now was to hold Pope at Manassas long enough for Lee and Longstreet to catch up. Then the two wings of the Rebel army could try to crush him between them.

Ironically, Pope thought that it was he who had Jackson trapped! He hurried his army toward Manassas, telling his men that "we shall bag the whole crowd." But his officers let him down, especially one or two loyal to McClellan, who would later be accused of intentionally dragging their feet. And then Jackson struck part of McDowell's corps in a devastating surprise attack near Groveton on the evening of August 28. The Yankees lost a third of their number, and had no choice but to retire a few miles to Manassas, where the main body of Pope's army gathered.

The Battle of Second Manassas began the next morning, August 29, and nothing worked out as

John Pope had hoped or expected. Deludedly thinking that the fight at Groveton had stopped Jackson in a vulnerable spot, Pope awoke believing that McDowell's corps would be in a position to swoop down on Stonewall and deliver a telling flank attack of its own. But McDowell was nowhere near where he was supposed to be, his command being scattered badly. Worse, Lee was only a few hours away as dawn approached, and moving fast.

The first shots were fired just after 5.30 a.m., when Sigel moved his command forward. Pope's army was spread out roughly along the old lines occupied by the Confederate army at the end of the first battle here on July 21, 1861. Ironically, the Confederates were occupying much the same position as that held by the attacking Federals in that first battle. Now Pope ordered Sigel to go forward, across the Warrenton Turnpike at Groveton, to strike Jackson's flank along an unfinished

railroad. Stonewall's men turned him back bloodily by late morning, and Sigel, ever timid, was already at the point of pulling back when his men saw a large body of Confederates approaching their exposed right flank on the turnpike. Lee and Longstreet had arrived.

Their arrival could not have been better timed or placed. Indeed, the Confederates won the first Manassas fight chiefly because of chance arrivals of fresh troops at precisely the right moment, and now history repeated itself, almost precisely on the same spot. But it took time for Lee and Longstreet to get on the field and set up their attack. Meanwhile, Pope occupied himself well into the afternoon with repeated attacks on Jackson in the railroad cut, to no avail. Pope expected McDowell and others to march around his left to take Jackson in flank, but they moved slowly and Pope waited in vain to hear the sounds of their striking Jackson. They never

ABOVE: The quiet, dusty, main street of Centreville, Virginia, presented much the same face as a hundred other Virginia villages. Yet the road running through it made the village important to the invasion or defense of northern Virginia. Though no battles were fought in its streets, battles were largely planned around control of the hamlet, and it figured prominently in two battles for Manassas.

LEFT: In March 1862 photographers came to Bull Run to record the ruins of the Stone Bridge on the Centreville-Warrenton pike, and the waters of Bull Run, soon to run red with blood once more.

did. Receiving word of Lee's arrival, McDowell stayed put until nightfall.

When the battle resumed the next day, Pope still believed he had the upper hand tactically, but his army was in a bad way for supplies, and no help was forthcoming from McClellan, who by now was back in Washington. Still, he believed that he had only Jackson facing him, and then by noon actually changed his mind to assert that the Confederates were now retreating! In fact, Pope was all along making erroneous deductions from misinterpreted intelligence, and did not get his attack going until about 3:00 p.m., giving Lee all the time he needed to rest his troops and make his plans.

Pope's renewed attack on the railroad cut was vicious, but Jackson's men repulsed assault after assault. Then McDowell, in immediate command, foolishly called for a division from the left flank, south of the Warrenton Turnpike, even though

reports were now coming in of a large enemy presence – Longstreet – in that area. As soon as the division had moved, Longstreet and half Lee's army struck. The effect was electric. The Confederates drove everything before them as the Federals, hit in the flank and rear, fell back almost in panic. Longstreet started to wheel his line to the left, like a book closing, with his own line the right half, and Jackson's the left, and the Yankees in the middle.

By late afternoon Pope had to admit that he was beaten. From there on it was a scramble to save his army. He had lost 14,500 killed, wounded, and captured, out of his 70,000-man army; Lee lost 9,400 of his 55,000. Three days later the campaign was over, Pope was defeated, the Union was in a panic, and Lee was ready to march into Maryland in his first invasion of the North. Twice witness to humiliating defeats for the North, Manassas would be an ill omen for Yankees for the rest of the war.

FACING PAGE: Men started erecting monuments even while the war raged. One of the very first was this red sandstone pyramid on Henry Hill, raised in memory of men who fell in the August 1862 battle and dedicated in June 1865, when hostile Confederates were still in the field in a few places.
ABOVE: The countryside around Centreville was turned into successive armed camps by both Blue and Gray. In March 1862 it looked like this after the Rebels evacuated. The Federals used much the same earthworks that summer, but never had to fight to defend them.

CHAPTER SEVENTEEN

GETTYSBURG

The ten months following Second Manassas were not good ones for the Union in the east. Lee's invasion of Maryland was turned back at Antietam by a timorous McClellan, who might have destroyed him had he the courage. But then at Fredericksburg in December, Lee delivered a costly defeat on the Rappahannock, and the following May, at nearby Chancellorsville, he made a shambles of several army corps, though at the cost of the loss of Stonewall Jackson. Out in the west the war went better, with control of the Mississippi gradually falling to the North. Still, all eyes were on the Army of the Potomac and the Army of Northern Virginia. And all asked

Gettysburg was the widowmaker. The Reb (top) in Devil's Den, the men of the III Corps and their officers (above), and gunners like the 5th U.S. Artillery (facing page), were savaged.

the same question. Could Lee ever be beaten? One man asking the question was General George G. Meade. He was placed in command of the Army of the Potomac at a crucial moment, on June 27, 1863. It was crucial because Lee was invading the North again, trying to take the war to the enemy and relieve the pressure on Virginia. He swept up through Maryland and into Pennsylvania, stealing a march on the Federals and leaving them racing to catch up with him and at the same time keep themselves between Lee and Washington. The pressure had been too much for Joseph Hooker, the discredited commander so badly beaten at Chancellorsville. He resigned without warning, and

Lincoln gave the command to Meade without even consulting him. No commander ever faced a greater challenge. Four days after assuming command, Meade would be fighting the greatest battle in the history of the hemisphere.

Lee was driving toward the Susquehanna River, and Pennsylvania's capital at Harrisburg. Meade had to prevent that, and drove hard to catch up to the Rebels. As fortune would have it, most of the major roads leading from several points in northern Maryland and central Pennsylvania converged at

TOP RIGHT: Brigadier General Alexander Hays was one of the many middle level commanders who performed admirably at Gettysburg. **ABOVE**: A. R. Waud's sketch of the fighting on the second day of the battle.
RIGHT: George A. Custer, his bright future before him, was with the cavalry at Gettysburg.
LEFT: An 1880s lithograph of the July 3 fighting.

the modest crossroads town of Gettysburg, thirty miles southeast of Harrisburg. Meade was approaching from the south, just as Lee, trying to concentrate his scattered columns, had elements of his I and III Corps moving toward the town. Neither general planned anything to take place there. Indeed, Meade expected that the coming battle would take place several miles distant, near a place called Pipe Creek. But on the morning of July 1, advance elements of General A.P. Hill's III Corps Rebels bumped into pickets from a Yankee cavalry brigade. With alarming rapidity the skirmish mushroomed into a major battle.

Both Lee and Meade realized that Gettysburg was a strategic crossroads and needed to be held. Each general, though many miles distant, began to rush troops toward the growing engagement. That first day, the advantage lay almost entirely with the Confederates. The Yankees were badly outnumbered, and tried only to fight a holding action until more help arrived. General John Reynolds strove bravely to maintain a defensive line, but then a marksman's bullet cut him down. Command devolved upon his next in line, General Abner Doubleday, the same man who fired the first Yankee shot at Fort Sumter. He was soon superseded by another senior general

FACING PAGE: Though staged, this post-battle image shows what the carnage in the Devil's Den looked like. ABOVE LEFT (inset): The Trostle house and barn just days after the battle, showing the destruction wreaked on men and animals alike. ABOVE RIGHT (inset): An artist's rendition of the scene at the Trostle house during the fight. ABOVE: A Reb who gave his all at Gettysburg.

BOTTOM: The third day of the battle opened with a scene much like this sketch by battlefield artist A. R. Waud. Troops rushed to the front, while others already there cooked their breakfast and waited for the big fight to come. On the hill crest at left center stands the position that Lee will attack in the grand assault.

RIGHT: The gatehouse of the Evergreen Cemetery on Cemetery Hill, the center of Meade's position, and the object of what would be called Pickett's Charge. It appears here just days after the battle. In fact, the attacking Confederates never reached it, as the painting (far right) might suggest. Still it conveys much of the sense of the scene as reinforcements rushed to assist in repelling the grandest assault of the war in the East. The line of smoke puffs in the distance marks the advance of the attackers, whose battle flags are dimly seen in Edwin Forbes' painting. But no painting could convey the bedlam of sound, smoke, and confusion, attendant to one of the few truly hand-to-hand conflicts of the Civil War.

as fresh troops arrived, but by 3:0 p.m. it looked black for them. Flanked on both sides by Hill's Confederates, with some of Richard Ewell's II Corps veterans now present, the Yankees were finally pushed back into the streets of Gettysburg itself, and beyond, taking up a last line of defense on Cemetery Hill, just south of the town. There they dug in, and there they stayed. They also found General Winfield Scott Hancock there, who now assumed command until Meade could arrive.

The rest of that day and all through the night more units arrived to bolster each army. Lee reached the field that afternoon, and Meade just before dawn on July 2. Looking at the ground, the Federals

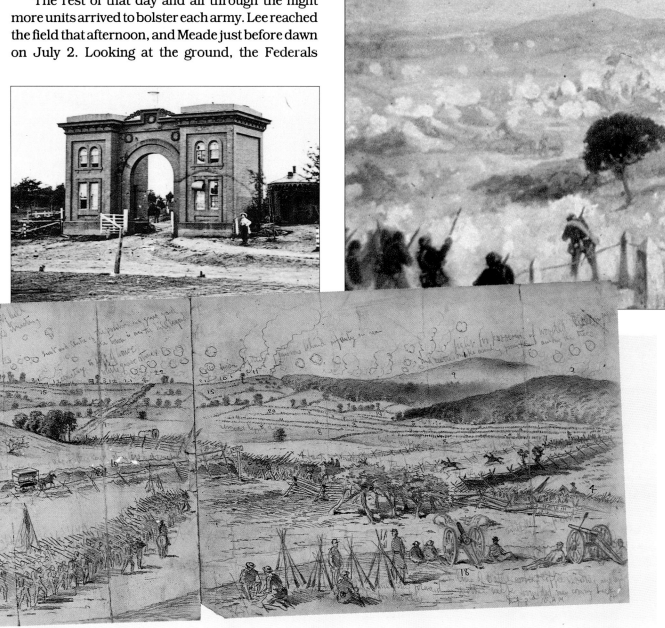

ABOVE: One of the older career soldiers who commanded the corps and divisions of the Army of the Potomac was Major General Erasmus D. Keyes, hardly inspired, but competent and dependable. BELOW: The tactical importance of Little Round Top is evident in Forbes' painting showing the commanding position that it gave to artillery.

made the best use of the advantage of position. A long, low elevation, Cemetery Ridge, extended southward from Cemetery Hill, and at the southern end sat a tall wooded knob, Little Round Top. More good ground curved eastward away from Cemetery Hill, to Culp's Hill. Meade placed his units along this line, forming the shape of an upside-down fishhook, and decided to stay on the defensive. It was a wise choice.

Lee had studied almost all through the night, talking with his commanders, to decide what to do. He had to attack while Meade's army was incomplete, that much he knew. He finally decided to strike at both ends of the Yankee line simultaneously, with Ewell making a supporting assault on Culp's Hill while Longstreet made the main attack at the opposite end of the Federal position, not far from Little Round Top.

Edwin Forbes left behind many poignant sketches made on the scene, depicting the cost of the battle on large scale and small. For more than an hour before Pickett's Charge, Rebel artillery bombarded the Union lines, seeking to silence its guns. **BELOW**: This was the aftermath: ruined guns and carriages, and slaughtered animals. Nevertheless, the Yankee artillery emerged relatively unscathed, to pour destruction on the assault.

At first, events seemed to favor Lee. One of Meade's subordinates, General Daniel Sickles, disobeyed his orders and put his III Corps, Meade's left flank, considerably in advance of the line chosen. When Longstreet struck these foolishly exposed troops, he almost destroyed Sickles' corps in an area called the Wheatfield. The battered remnant fell back to the proper line, with the Confederates swinging around and making for Little Round Top. If they took it and put cannon on its crest, they could shell the entire Union line on Cemetery Ridge and force Meade to withdraw. Fortunately, a last

RIGHT: Elon J. Farnsworth never got to wear the stars of a general. Promoted just before the battle, he was killed leading his cavalry brigade in the sideshow cavalry fighting that took place a few miles from the main battlefield on July 3.
FAR RIGHT: A battlefield artist's more finished watercolor sketch of the climactic fighting of July 3. It depicts the moment when the Confederates briefly struck and broke through the Union lines. The officer just going down while holding the flag at left center may be Armistead

: On the back slope of Cemetery Ridge, a mute cannon stands where once hundreds repelled the great attack. Meade sits astride "Old Baldy" where he watched the final fury of the battle, and all along the crest monuments proclaim the moment of glory of the Union's sons. LEFT: It was a melancholy procession of Confederates who turned their backs to the foe and marched back toward Virginia after the defeat. Forbes left this impression of the Army of Northern Virginia on its retreat toward the Potomac. Nearly a third of their comrades were casualties, and Lee's army would never be entirely the same again.

minute scramble saw Federals get to the summit first and, despite bitter attacks from the foe, the bluecoats held Little Round Top. At the other end of the line, Ewell bungled his Culp's Hill attack.

Meade's line held firm. That night he decided to remain on the defensive, anticipating that Lee's next attack the following day, July 3, would come in the center. He was quite right. Lee, exasperated, could think of nothing else to do. He ordered feints on the flanks of the Federal line, but planned a massive artillery bombardment aimed at the center, on Cemetery Ridge. If he could break through the enemy center, he could roll up either or both halves of the Yankee army.

The bombardment started at 1:0 p.m. and continued for two hours, but most of the shells went wide of their marks, doing no damage. Then Longstreet gave the order for George Pickett's Virginia division and James Pettigrew's North Carolina division to go forward in the grandest frontal assault of the war. "Pickett's Charge," as it would be called, saw the brave Rebels march across a mile of open fields and up into the face of the Yankee rifles and artillery on Cemetery Ridge. It was a doomed effort from the start, but done with incredible gallantry. None broke through, and more than a third never got back.

With the failure of the attack, Lee admitted defeat, and soon started to retreat back toward Virginia. He had lost more than 20,000 of the 70,000 men in his army, while Meade suffered 23,000 out of 90,000. The North was safe, and Lee would never lead another offensive. The tide of the war was turning.

ABOVE: Many of Lee's men – 3,000 of them – would never cross the Potomac again. Like these dead, they lay in rows where they fell or were dragged by the burial parties.

CHAPTER EIGHTEEN
ATLANTA

ABOVE: U.S. Grant, the man who planned the road to victory, left the vital task of subduing the enemy army in Georgia to his most able subordinate William T. Sherman (facing page).

Gettysburg was not the only turning point. The day after Lee's defeat, U.S. Grant finally took Vicksburg on the Mississippi. With it he split the Confederacy in two. That fall a Union army took Chattanooga, nearly lost it again after the Battle of Chickamauga, but then survived being besieged to break out and drive the Confederate Army of Tennessee back into north Georgia. That winter Grant was made general-in-chief of all Northern armies, and he set in motion a plan to press the Rebels at all points at once. Meade would advance into Virginia and go after Lee, and the main western armies, led by William Tecumseh Sherman, would go after Atlanta, Georgia, the South's last major supply and communications center linking the Confederacy east and west. If he could take it, Sherman would split the eastern Confederacy in two.

In early May 1864 Sherman started his campaign, and during the ensuing three months he steadily forced his foe to retreat before him. The Confederate Army of Tennessee, commanded by General Joseph E. Johnston, took a defensive posture from the beginning, in part because it was outnumbered, and in part also because Johnston did not have the moral courage to risk an all-out battle. In a series of engagements – Rocky Face Ridge, Resaca, Cassville, New Hope Church,

BOTTOM (inset): Side-by-side, General Hood's Confederate headquarters sits quietly in the distance, while the foreground reveals newer Federal defenses erected after the Rebels evacuated Atlanta. BELOW (inset): Another view in Atlanta's environs, showing remains of a Confederate fort on Peachtree Street.

FACING PAGE (inset): Another Confederate fort on the Marietta Road, north of Atlanta. Most of these forts never actually saw action, for Hood's attacks in July, and the Battle of Jonesboro weeks later, sealed the city's fate without Sherman having to assault its defenses.

MAIN PICTURE: A dramatic view of the Confederate lines east of Atlanta, showing the ruins of a railroad line, and a locomotive with no cars left to pull. Chimneys show where houses once stood, idle wheels all that remains of boxcars. The scenes of destruction were repeated again and again.

BELOW: General H. Thomas, slow but dependable, was one of Sherman's instruments in driving Johnston through Georgia to Atlanta.
RIGHT: At New Hope Church, as everywhere else, Johnston offered only defensive works to the enemy, battling Sherman with wood and earth, but little of brilliance or courage on his own part, forcing President Davis to replace him.

RIGHT: When Davis put Hood in charge, it was already too late. Atlanta, its rail depot shown here, was virtually surrounded by the Yankee army. The Confederates had built miles of earthworks and fortifications around the city, like those shown on the facing page; trenches backed by more trenches, with lines of sharpened stakes, abatis, even wire, strung out in advance to deter any attackers. But Sherman did not need to attack, he had only to cut their supply lines and starve them out or force their retreat.

Kennesaw Mountain – Johnston offered only delaying actions, and then withdrew. Only at Kennesaw Mountain did he give Sherman a sound beating, when the Federals unwisely launched precipitate attacks against a well-defended position.

By July Johnston had reached Peachtree Creek, less than five miles from Atlanta itself. By now President Jefferson Davis was exasperated with a general who seemed never to have things sufficiently to his liking to stand and give battle. When Johnston could offer no statement of his plans for defending the city, Davis relieved him of command. Many have since charged Davis with a dreadful mistake in relieving Johnston, but there is no reason to suppose that the general would have done anything but keep retreating if left in charge. Davis' real error, however, was in appointing General John B. Hood as replacement. There was no question of Hood being a bold fighter. He had also intrigued to get the command. But he simply was not smart enough to lead an army.

Fearing that he must act decisively and quickly, Hood ordered an attack just three days after

assuming command. On July 20 he launched the Battle of Peachtree Creek, sending the two corps under Generals William J. Hardee and A.P. Stewart forward to attack George H. Thomas' Army of the Cumberland – one of three so-called armies within Sherman's overall command. Hood hoped to catch Thomas in the open and away from support by other Federal forces. Unfortunately, Thomas proved too stubborn, and Hood proved too weak a manager. The fighting was inconclusive, and when the Confederates withdrew that evening they had suffered casualties almost three times those of the Federals.

But Hood was not to be stopped with one defeat. Two days later he swung Hardee and the corps of Benjamin F. Cheatham around to the east of Atlanta to meet the advancing Federal Army of the Tennessee led by General James McPherson. What followed was the Battle of Atlanta, and once again Hood did not run it well. Cheatham's attack was badly managed and dreadfully late, and when night fell and the Confederates pulled back, they had suffered double the enemy's losses, a fact only redeemed in part by the death of McPherson, the only Yankee

LEFT: An early lithograph offering a melodramatic view of Sherman's "bummers" starting the destruction of Georgia's war materiel. TOP: Sherman's chief of artillery, General William F. Barry, who oversaw much of the neutralization of Confederate works, like those (above) on Peachtree Street in Atlanta.

RIGHT: Two Pennsylvanians who served through the Atlanta Campaign. Brothers, the one at left, Frederick Cordes, fought with the 190th Pennsylvania. Henry, on the right, was in the 18th U.S. Infantry, and lost his left arm at Jonesboro in the last fight before the fall of Atlanta. Both were members of the "Bucktails," Pennsylvania regiments that wore the distinctive deer tail in their hats.

army commander to be killed in battle.

Six days later Hood struck west of Atlanta at McPherson's forces once more, now commanded by General John Schofield. The Battle of Ezra Church only made matters worse. Hood was not on the field – as he had not been during the previous battles – and Schofield's men fought brilliantly. This time Hood's casualties were more than ten times his opponents', and for it he gained nothing. Hood was rapidly destroying his own army.

Throughout August Sherman shelled Atlanta and its defenses, while remaining content not to attack Hood's defenses. Instead, he steadily spread his own lines out, encircling the city and cutting off its railroad communications. By the end of the month, Hood was almost encircled, and tried one last attack, at Jonesboro, twelve miles south of Atlanta, where Sherman threatened to cut the last line. It was another bungled affair, with Hood again absent from the field, and his poor, battered veterans had little fight left in them. The Federals crushed and almost surrounded the Rebels, and took Jonesboro handily. With it gone, all hope of holding Atlanta dissolved, and on September 1 Hood began evacuating the city. "Atlanta is ours," Sherman could wire headquarters,

TOP: The work of destruction of machinery and stores in captured Atlanta commences, as the depots and machinery of the railroad is dismantled or burned.

ABOVE: Boilers, rails, ties, everything related to Confederate transportation, is destroyed.

LEFT: "Sherman's hairpins," they called the twisted iron rails left in the wake of the Yankees' passing. Special tools were made to bend and ruin the red-hot rails, heated over their own burning ties.

CHAPTER NINETEEN

PETERSBURG

The Confederacy was tottering on its knees, everyone could see that. But it was still dangerous. Sherman had not completely crushed Hood. He still had to carry out his March to the Sea to take Savannah and finish splitting the lower South. And even as he occupied Atlanta and sent his victory telegram, his commander, Grant, was facing becoming mired down in one of the longest sieges in history in Virginia.

After Gettysburg, Meade remained in command of the Army of the Potomac, but it would be ten months before it met Lee again in a major contest. The armies feinted through the rest of 1863, then rested and refitted during the winter. In May 1864,

Petersburg was a matter of cannon and fortifications. Batteries like the one at top pounded away at the log and earth works (facing page), while miles of abatis separated the lines.

as Union armies advanced everywhere, Meade moved into an area called the Wilderness, below the Rappahannock, and inaugurated six weeks of almost constant combat, with Grant present in person to supervise. The armies grappled inconclusively through the Wilderness, on to Spotsylvania, then Cold Harbor. By early June Grant and Meade were east of Richmond, roughly where McClellan had been in 1862, but Lee was well entrenched in front of them and could not be budged.

Then Grant conceived the idea of removing his whole army from Lee's front, undetected, and marching south to the James River, crossing over speedily-erected pontoon bridges, then moving a

BELOW: The James River was the greatest geographical obstacle to Union movement, but not great enough to stop Grant, who stole a march on Lee, built a pontoon bridge, and moved his army across it and to the very suburbs of Petersburg before Lee knew what had happened.

few miles west to Petersburg. This city, twenty-five miles south of Richmond, was its key, controlling all but one of the vital rail lines that fed the Confederate Capital. Take Petersburg, and Richmond must fall.

Grant's movement was executed brilliantly. It was almost impossible to fool Lee, but for fully a day Grant left him bewildered, and by June 15 elements

TOP RIGHT: Major General William F. Smith passed by one of the greatest opportunities of the war when he dallied on June 15 instead of aggressively assaulting Petersburg when it was so weakly held it must have fallen to him. Instead, it became a siege war by spade and ax and earth.

RIGHT: Here gabions are being made of sticks, to be filled with dirt for fortifications.

of the Army of the Potomac were on the south side of the James, marching toward a virtually undefended Petersburg. The commander there had but 2,200 men, facing 15,000 in Grant's advance. But that commander was the plucky General Beauregard, hero of Fort Sumter. When the Federals approached, he hastily gathered every spare man, even clerks and shop-keepers, to man his defenses. Then, to Grant's eternal frustration, the Yankee commander on the scene, General W.F. Smith, took his time about attacking, and did not do so until almost dark. If he had moved quickly he could have taken Petersburg. By stalling, he helped prolong the war for another ten months.

Lee sped reinforcements to Petersburg when Beauregard sent word of the threat, and when more determined Yankee attacks came forth on the next and following days, the Rebels managed to repel them. By June 19 Grant realized that all the benefits of his brilliant surprise had been squandered. Lee was ready. There was nothing to do but rest the men after their long campaign, dig earthworks, and commence a siege.

Thus it became a war of spades and shovels for several weeks. With his right anchored on the Appomattox River just to the east of Petersburg, Grant would gradually extend his left below and around the city over the following months, all the

ABOVE: In yet another of Grant's attempts to take the Rebels by surprise, a tunnel was dug between the lines and tons of powder exploded beneath a salient in the Confederate works. The blast created this "crater," into which thousands poured in the unsuccessful attempt to breach the Southern lines.

LEFT: Major General Horatio G. Wright of the VI Corps was one of many Yankee high commanders who suffered the boredom of the siege that followed, with only occasional reassignment for variety.

ABOVE: The attack on the Crater was a fiasco for a number of reasons, not least the timidity of the man sitting at center, General Edward Ferrero. Instead of being with his troops and overseeing their advance after the explosion, he was cowering far in the rear, apparently looking to his own safety first. Nevertheless, he posed confidently with his staff just days after the event, giving no sign that he had ruined his career and cost the lives of hundreds.

RIGHT: Taking a cue from the Yankees, the Rebels, too, commenced tunnels and laying mines. This one was discovered in April 1865 after Petersburg's fall, still incomplete. Called the "Mahone Mine," it, like several others, was evidence of wishful thinking more than concerted tactical planning, and not one Rebel mine was exploded.

while facing a formidable line of defenses erected two years before by the enemy, and now considerably strengthened. There were no battles, and few skirmishes, as the combatants glowered at each other across the lines. Instead, a kind of boredom set in, and the men turned their minds to inventive means of ending the tedium. Thus it was that coal miners in the 48th Pennsylvania Infantry proposed the idea of digging a tunnel from their lines, across to and under the enemy defenses. They would then place a massive charge of gunpowder there, detonate it, and blow a hole in Lee's works, through which the Federals could attack. Grant adopted the idea, in part just to give his men something to do. The work took more than a month, but finally on July 30 all was ready. When the fuze was lit, at first it went out and had to be relit. The resulting explosion blew tens of tons of earth, ramparts, wooden breastworks, cannon, and Confederates, hundreds of feet into the air. But Grant had entrusted the follow-up attack to Generals Ambrose Burnside, James Ledlie,

and Edward Ferrero – a bungler, a drunkard, and a coward respectively. They botched the whole affair, and the result was thousands of casualties and nothing to show for it. Lee held his lines, and the siege went on.

Grant could only keep slowly extending his lines, while making cavalry raids to keep Lee off balance. But the best cavalry raid came from Lee. His cavalry commander, General Wade Hampton, learned that a herd of 2,000 beeves was quartered several miles in rear of Grant's army. In mid-September Hampton sent 4,000 troopers on a daring enterprise to ride clear around the enemy lines and into his rear, to capture the herd and drive it back to Petersburg and its defenders' hungry mouths. It

was a brilliant success that even the Federals had to admire. But it was nothing compared to Grant's steady gains as he cut off one railroad after another. Throughout the fall and into the winter of 1864-5, the Federals continued to lengthen their noose around Lee. There was a score of small engagements, but each ended with the inevitable expansion of Yankee control. Finally, on March 25, Lee authorized a surprise attack calculated to take a key section of the Union works, force Grant to shorten his lines temporarily, and thus allow Lee to get his army and its equipment out of the lines. Petersburg would have to be abandoned, but at least he could save his army. The attack started successfully at first, but it could not sustain its momentum.

TOP: Petersburg, and especially the Crater fiasco, was finally the end of the line for a commander who had been ill-starred throughout the war. Ambrose Burnside had commanded the Army of the Potomac once, but he would be best known to posterity for giving his name to a style of whiskers. ABOVE LEFT: Reconstructed "bomb proofs" at Petersburg give evidence of soldier wit even in the most trying circumstances, dubbing a rude earth hole the "Willard Hotel."

ABOVE: A. R. Waud's on-the-spot drawing of sharpshooters from the XVIII Corps, coolly firing from their works and picking off Rebels on the other side who were foolish enough to expose themselves.
RIGHT: Jubilant Yankees stand fearlessly atop the works for the first time in April 1865, after the Confederates have pulled out and Petersburg has fallen.

Now it was only a matter of time, and on April 1 the western end of Lee's defensive line collapsed. The Army of Northern Virginia had only hours to get out. On April 2 the evacuation began, a brilliant and desperate rearguard action holding back thousand of attacking Federals while Lee raced westward. Later that same day the Yankees entered Petersburg. The next morning they walked into an undefended Richmond.

The war still had a few weeks to go. One week later Grant brought Lee to bay at Appomattox, where, unable to move in any direction, he was forced to surrender. Sherman had marched to the

RIGHT: The quiet village of Appomattox Courthouse sleeps today as it did in 1865, when the armies came reeling across the Virginia landscape to have their final meeting here, not to make war, but to start the peace. Ironically, Lee and Grant made their terms in the parlor of Wilmer McLean, who had lived alongside Bull Run in 1861, but left to get away from the war. It found him one more time.

BELOW: The ultimate price of the war came in the blood and lives that it cost. This Confederate, killed in the last week of the war at Petersburg, was only one of more than a quarter million Southerners who gave their lives for the cause they espoused. Like these dead (facing page) at Petersburg, they mingled their blood with that of 300,000 Yankee dead, to nurture the soil of a troubled, but reunited, nation.

sea the previous winter, taking Savannah, Georgia in December, then starting a destructive march northward through the Carolinas. Davis had put Johnston back in command of the remnants of the Confederate armies in the region, including the remainder of the Army of Tennessee which Hood had led to near-fatal disaster against Thomas at Nashville in December. But Johnston could do nothing, and he, too, surrendered late in April. With that, the Civil War was virtually over.

Behind them all lay those 10,000 fights, engagements as diverse as an attack on a massive brick fort, iron monsters shooting at each other on the water, lightning virtually striking twice in the same spot called Manassas, the massive conflagration of Gettysburg, a city that became a battleground in Georgia, and the longest siege of the war. It was all a part of the indescribable tragedy of an era when Americans turned the land that they all loved into a battlefield.

THE WEAPONS

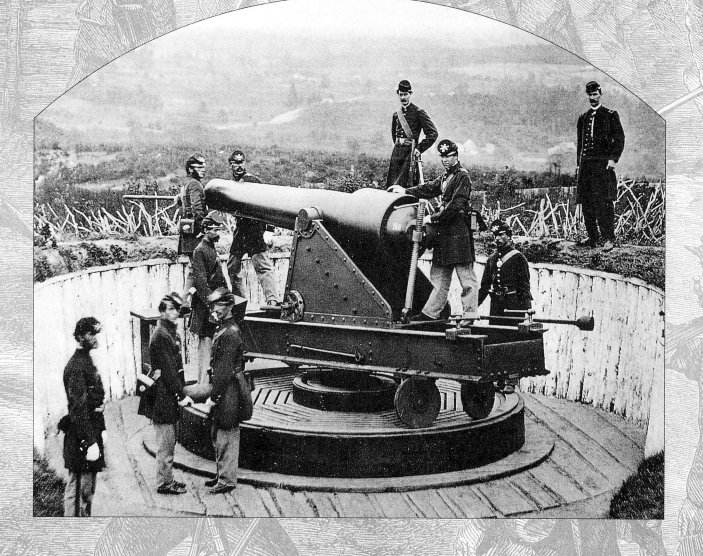

ABOVE: Fort Totten, one of the host of works ringing Washington, boasted this massive 100-pounder Parrott rifle in 1865.

THE WEAPONS

E very war is a partnership of two otherwise very dissimilar elements, one quite animate, the other very much inanimate. But when brought together, they make battlefields terrible and determine the fate of nations. One, of course, is the soldier. Without him there would be no armies. And the other is the weapon, for without it the armies could do no more than fight with their fists.

When America went to war with itself in 1861, the state of technology in the production and development of military weapons had only recently entered a new phase, one that would catapult warfare itself into the modern world. Many, especially those in high positions of responsibility, still looked

to the weapons of the past, not yet aware of the revolution that technology would soon bring about. Thus weapons as old as warfare itself, many virtually unchanged for thousands of years, would be put into the hands of the young men who went to America's battlefields.

But at the same time there would be other, frighteningly new and deadly things on those fields, weapons capable of a level and scale of destruction barely dreamed of only a generation before; weapons that would help to make the Civil War the bloodiest single conflict in American history. Thanks to these messengers of death, the single day's fighting at Antietam in September 1862 would see more Americans lose their lives than in the massive invasion of Normandy on D-Day. Thanks to these weapons, more Americans would die in the Civil War than in all of the rest of the nation's wars combined, from the colonial wars through Korea.

LEFT: Every kind of weapon that came into a soldier's hands is evident in the lithograph at left: rifles, pistols, swords, bayonets, knives, and cannon. It was a fearful arsenal.

CHAPTER TWENTY
EDGED WEAPONS

There is probably only one weapon whose history goes back farther in time than the sword and the lance, and that would be the stone. To be sure, there were occasions during the Civil War when soldiers, out of ammunition, actually threw rocks at their foes, but no one ever formally planned a role for such missiles in the conflict. For edged weapons, however, the story was very much different.

For millenia soldiers had terrified their foes with sharp-edged, bright polished blades, gleaming in rank upon rank just before the attack, and promising painful, bloody battle. By the Middle Ages most foot soldiers no longer carried swords,

ABOVE: The bayonet dated back as long as shoulder arms, and even further into antiquity, to pikes and spears. FACING PAGE: Every soldier had a bayonet, but very few used them.

those being reserved for commanders and mounted forces. Instead, the man in the ranks carried a pike or lance, little more than a short sword at the end of a pole, literally extending the reach of his arm. Incredibly, centuries later, in 1861, some men still went to war with this, and nothing more.

In 1861, when the 6th Pennsylvania Cavalry was enlisted under its colonel, Richard Rush, the troopers were equipped with standard cavalry sabers, pistols ... and nine-foot-long Norway fir lances with triangular edged iron spikes at the tips. But for their uniforms and pistols, these Pennsylvanians would not have looked out of place on the fields of Cannae or on the plains

BELOW: Whenever the officers posed, they had their sabers by their sides, like these men of General Orlando B. Willcox' staff in August 1864. Willcox sits second from the right beneath an impromptu sun shelter that soldiers called a "shebang."

of Marathon. A few other mounted regiments, especially in the Confederate army, also carried pikes, chiefly because they could not obtain better weapons, but every unit that could, soon abandoned such medieval trappings for weapons more in keeping with the war at hand.

Rush's Lancers, as they were called, were only an extreme example of the backward-looking logic that dominated military thinking on both sides early in the war. Few high officials in Washington or

RIGHT: Just a few of the edged weapons that went off to war with Reb and Yank. The sword at bottom is a standard U.S. cavalry saber from before the war, though such models continued to see use. Above it is an engraved, privately manufactured saber, no doubt carried by an officer. The knife, sometimes called a "sheath" or "Bowie," is definitely not government issue.

Richmond fully appreciated the fact that the invention of the percussion lock, rifling in gun barrels, and the conical Minie bullet, made virtually all previous forms of weapons obsolete. This applied especially to edged weapons, which were only effective on a face-to-face, hand-to-hand basis, whereas the rifled bullet could deliver injury or death more than a quarter-mile from its sender. Unfortunately, it remained for soldiers in blue and gray to discover this for themselves, and to pay for the revelation with their blood.

While lances appeared only briefly, and disappeared quickly, a near cousin, in concept at

BELOW: Colonel Arthur Herbert of the 17th Virginia Infantry presents a typical picture of the Confederate field officer with his sword at his side. The blade may have seen Old Army service before the war, or it may be of Southern manufacture, for the Confederates soon put an effective industrial operation together to manufacture edged weapons.

least, remained on the battlefields throughout the war. The bayonet appeared more than a century earlier, at a time when flintlock muskets were cumbersome, slow in firing, and woefully inaccurate. Theory called for the firing of a volley or two, creating more smoke and noise than damage, and then a spirited assault, trusting to the gleaming bayonets at the muzzles of the guns to do the real work, making the blade yet again just an extension of the infantryman's arm.

It was sound thinking given the state of shoulder arms in the eighteenth century. Failing to appreciate the impact of the rifle on this, however, commanders going into the Civil War assumed that the same

tactics should apply. Literally without exception, every properly equipped infantryman on both sides, perhaps as many as two million men in all, carried bayonets of varying size and description. Their variety was almost bewildering. The average bayonet was eighteen inches or more in length, triangular in cross section, and tapering to a sharp point, with deep grooves between its edges. Some, however, were much shorter, little more than knives, while others stretched up to two feet from the muzzle of a rifle. Some, like the saber bayonet used with model 1853 British Short rifles, were literally swords. The British Brunswick saber actually resembled an ancient Roman short sword more than anything

ABOVE: A well-outfitted Yankee company poses for the camera, bayonets in place, and their captain standing before them, sword drawn, ready for the mostly ceremonial function of holding it over his head to signal the charge.
RIGHT: A Confederate officer in ersatz uniform, holding an ivory-gripped presentation saber probably given to him by admiring townsfolk back home.

FAR LEFT: Union Major General Robert H. Milroy, wearing the old pre-war sword and scabbard with no frills.

The variety of blades that went to war was seemingly infinite, reflecting the highly idiosyncratic nature of the men themselves, and the relative indifference of the governments to absolute uniformity, most especially in the Confederacy, which was glad to have any weapon, regardless of its pattern or manufacturer. None of these is of government issue from either side.

else, as did a number of the improvised bayonets manufactured in the Confederacy. Union infantrymen carrying the Model 1855 saber bayonet actually wore a scabbard on their belts.

In the very first major engagement of the war, at Bull Run in 1861, commanders expected the bayonet, not the bullet, to win the day. General Thomas J. Jackson won his immortal sobriquet "Stonewall" on that field, only minutes after telling another Confederate officer, "Sir, we'll give them the bayonet" when the Federals were attacking. "Trust to the bayonet," Jackson said a little later as his men went into action.

ABOVE: One of the innumerable idealized lithographs showing the people back home what war was supposed to look like, with soldiers in serried ranks advancing bravely with an iron line of bayonets before them. While bayonets managed to instill some fear in a foe from time to time, they rarely inflicted any wounds, being reserved for use as candlesticks and roasting spits.

Yet the men never did trust their bayonets, nor, with very few exceptions, did they ever have occasion to use them as intended. Bayonet practice during drill struck many as ludicrous, going through the manual of instructions, and looking, as one Yankee said, like "a line of beings made up about equally of the frog, the sand-hill crane, the sentinel crab, and the grasshopper: all of them rapidly jumping, thrusting, swinging, striking, jerking every which way, and all gone stark mad."

Despite all the intent and orders of their commanders, most Civil War soldiers never came to actual hand-to-hand fighting, and therefore never

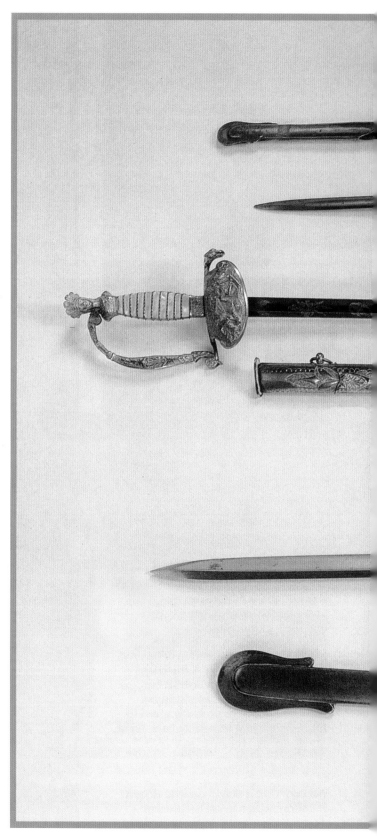

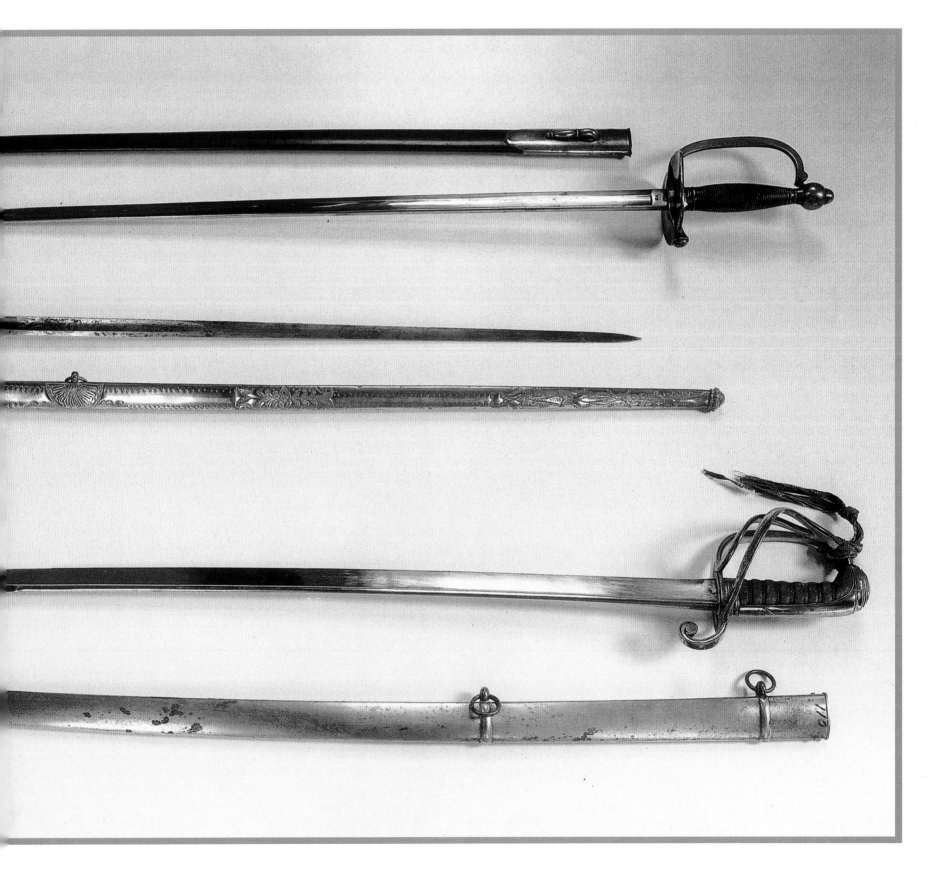

RIGHT: Major General A. A. Humphries and staff, with their swords, pose for the camera outside Washington in June 1865, with their war over. It is a safe bet that the only wounds ever inflicted during the war by these blades were accidental, either to the owners themselves or their horses. **FAR RIGHT:** service branches had different blades, like the medical corps sword of Surgeon Samuel W. Crawford.

ABOVE: Both North and South there were a number of pre-war, privately raised and funded militia groups that brought their uniforms and weapons to war with them. Outfits like the Washington Artillery of New Orleans, some of its officers shown here around 1861, often carried horrible looking sabers nearly as big as the men themselves, and far too unwieldy to serve more than ceremonial use.

used their bayonets in combat. Instead, they jammed them in the ground at their bivouacs or into the walls of their winter huts, finding that the socket designed to attach the bayonet to the muzzle of a gun was ideal for holding a candle. More often still a bayonet, this time attached to the rifle, made a perfect spit for roasting some poor farmer's chicken or ham over an open campfire.

If the bayonet proved ineffective, the sword, in all its varieties, was even less useful in this war. With the exception of a few regiments, mostly Confederate, that carried Bowie knives, only cavalry units were issued with sabers. Some artillery batteries equipped their cannoneers with weapons like the Roman-looking Model 1833 Foot Artillery short sword. And, of course, all officers were authorized to carry sabers at their belts. The selection among such weapons was even greater than with the bayonets. Some were ancient, like the

Revolutionary War sword that Confederate General Joseph E. Johnston wore into battle. Others were massive, perhaps the largest being a ten-pound monster carried by Major Heros von Borke. Many, especially those worn by non-combatant staff officers, were little more than ceremonial, and too lightweight for actual use.

The great majority of swords in use by both armies were based upon standard patterns issued in the old United States Army before the war. The Model 1840 and Model 1860 cavalry sabers predominated among bluecoat horsemen, and a great many Confederates carried them as well, after picking them up from the battlefield or taking them from captured Yankees. Dozens of varying patterns were manufactured by Confederate makers, but the basic design differed very little, almost all being sharp on the front edge, blunt on the back, with so-called "blood grooves" running down the sides, and

"three-bar" brass grip guards. Officers carried the Model 1840 cavalry saber or the lighter Model 1841 light artillery saber, though many commanders, especially in the Confederacy, brought their own blades from home, or bought them from private makers like the Ames company of Chicopee, Massachusetts. In the Union Navy, cutlasses of the 1841 or 1860 pattern were used, though rarely, and only occasionally actually worn by seamen.

Officers and enlisted men alike agreed upon one thing. Whatever variety of sword they used, and wherever it came from, the thing was practically useless. Officers rarely put theirs to any better purpose than holding it over their heads for the men to see and rally around during an attack, or else as a tool to threaten wavering men back into the ranks. For cavalrymen it was much the same. Indeed, most eventually acquired a disdain for their long blades, and many a trooper either left it behind

FAR LEFT: A post-war lithograph of the Battle of Nashville shows a host of blades and their uses, including as flagpoles. **LEFT:** An officer's ceremonial sword, scabbard, and sash, together with an artilleryman's blade based on the Roman short sword. **BELOW:** Admiral Silas Stringham wears a Union naval officer's blade.

when going into battle – trusting to his pistol and carbine – or else discarded it altogether. "The saber is of no use against gunpowder," declared the dashing Rebel raider John S. Mosby, while one of the troopers in Confederate General John Hunt Morgan's famous cavalry asserted that, after 1862, any man seen carrying a sword "would be forever after a laughing stock for the entire command." The cavalrymen did far more damage to themselves and to their own horses than they ever inflicted upon enemies with their blades. No wonder that almost all swords finally saw only the same limited service given to bayonets. As Mosby put it, "the only real use I ever heard of their being put to was to hold a piece of meat over the fire."

In the end there could be little more eloquent testimony to the obsolescence of edged weapons in warfare by the time of the Civil War than the fact that out of the millions of wounds inflicted between 1861 and 1865, only four-tenths of one percent – four out of every thousand – were inflicted by a sword or bayonet.

SHOULDER ARMS

What relegated edged weapons to such an insignificant role were the developments that had revolutionized firearms. Two generations before the Civil War, slow flintlock firing mechanisms and smoothbore musket barrels ensured that a soldier could only get off one shot every couple of minutes, and that when he did, the bullet would not go far, nor would it be likely to hit its target. The development of the percussion system, in which a copper cap could be quickly placed over a nipple at the breech, sending a spark into the powder charge when struck by the hammer, meant that three or more shots per minute could be fired. Moreover, the use of rifling grooves inside the barrel, imparting gyroscopic "spin" to the bullet as it exited, increased both the range and accuracy of the projectile, especially once the French Minie bullet was introduced. Its hollow base expanded upon firing, gripping the rifling effectively, while its cylindroconoidal shape kept it steady in flight.

All of these developments were available in military firearms by the 1840s, though the U.S. Army was

LEFT: A Union soldier in full field equipment, with a rare Sharps infantry rifle and bayonet. Few regiments were armed with this weapon. FACING PAGE: An examiner's report on tests of the Johnson breech-loading carbine.

393

EXPERIMENTS ON SMALL ARMS, (CLASS 6.)

(1) Report on Johnsons B.L. Carbine with Rowes Improvement
made by Wm Prince 2nd Lieut at Washington Arsenal 1864.
Mar 12th

Received at Ordnance Office,
March 11 1864.

CONSTRUCTION DIVISION.

Book ~~C.R.~~, Letter ~~H~~, No. ~~41~~
~~E.X. 6 – 306.~~

Ex.—6—393

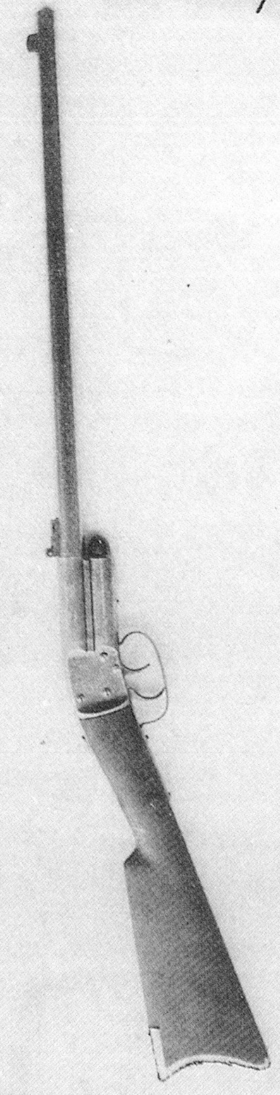

CLOSED

Washington Arsenal
March 14th 1864.

Capt J. G. Benton Ordn Dept
Comdg Washington Arsenal

Sir

In accordance with your orders I have subjected Johnsons B.L. Carbine with Rowes Improvement to a trial against the Standard Sharpes Carbine and have the honor to submit the following Report

Description of the Piece

It appears from the statement of Mr Johnson that the kind of Carbine in question has been already tried and reported on at this Arsenal, and that the objection urged against it was the difficulty encountered in extracting the case of the Cartridge after firing, which objection he claims to be removed by the Rowe improvement. As, however, no record of such trial appears upon the books of the Arsenal it may be well to repeat the description of the arm.

The general appe...

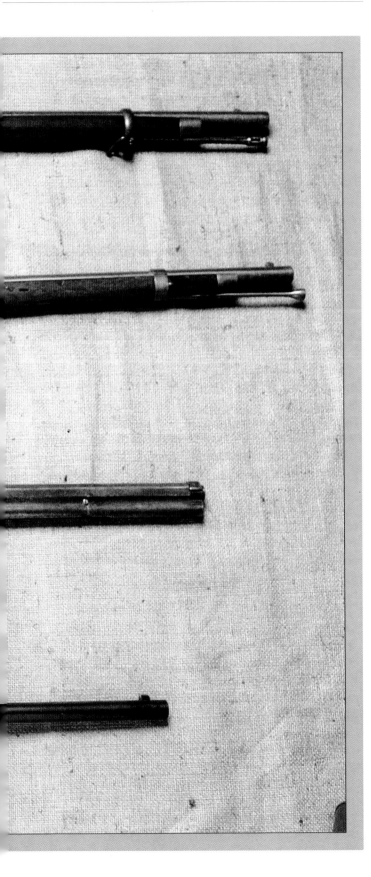

slow to adopt them on a wide scale, distrusting the marksmanship of the average soldier – with good reason – and fearing that the potential increase in the rate of fire would only lead to soldiers wasting more ammunition. Still, by 1861 almost all standard issue shoulder arms in the army were rifled, percussion lock weapons.

In the Union Army, throughout the war, the weapon of choice, and the one most widely used, was the Springfield, named for the armory at Springfield, Massachusetts, and available in several models. Indeed, it was not much different from the Model 1841 Harpers Ferry Rifle, only longer and with a larger bore. Adaptations were made in an 1855 model, and then, with the U.S. Model 1861 rifle-musket, the true Springfield emerged. It was 55.75 inches long, weighed 8.88 pounds, and was bored for a .58 caliber Minie bullet. It was simple, hardy, could be fired three times a minute or more, with a full charge of black powder it could be deadly effective at 300 yards or further, and with a lucky shot could still down a man at a range of half a mile. It cost between $18 and $25 to manufacture, and in the end the Union bought or made more than 1,470,000 of them.

The soldiers who carried them loved the Springfields. They were lighter than many of the imported rifles first issued to regiments, more accurate, and did not "kick" as much when fired. Indeed, even Confederates favored the weapon, anxious to pick them up on the battlefield or appropriate them from captured Yankees. Confederate manufacturers made copies of the Springfield, most notably the Richmond rifle. In the end, more Springfields, in several variants including copies, were made than any other percussion rifle ever used in America. It was the zenith of its type, and the last percussion muzzle-loader adopted by Washington before the conversion to breech-loaders.

Before the Model 1861 got into full production, many Union regiments were armed with British Enfield rifles, and this same weapon was to be the backbone of the Confederate infantry's armament. Only slightly smaller in bore, at .577 caliber, two inches shorter and several ounces lighter, it performed just as well as the Springfield, and some maintained better. Confederate authorities bought

LEFT: A few of the superb weapons used by Johnny Reb and Billy Yank. The .577 Enfield is at top, and beneath it is the .58 Springfield, the workhorses of Blue and Gray infantry. The brassblocked Henry rifle is below, a major step forward in weapon design and used mostly by infantry, while at bottom sits the 1859 Sharps carbine, issued almost exclusively to the cavalry.

ABOVE: A Yankee soldier demonstrates positions from the manual of arms with his pre-war model U.S. infantry rifle, intending to show how manageable the weapon could be despite its size.

and brought through the blockade more than 120,000 of them during the war, at the same time manufacturing home-grown copies. In conforming with the widespread use of Enfields throughout its armies, the Confederate government adopted .577 as the official caliber for all shoulder weapons, where possible.

Though these two rifles dominated battlefields North and South, the fact is that, even with the numbers in use combined, the two together still only accounted for a minority of the muskets and rifles used in the war. More than a hundred different models saw some kind of use, especially at the beginning of the conflict when many regiments armed themselves and men brought their own weapons from home, and toward the end in the Confederate service, when hard-pressed Rebels fought with any sort of gun they could find.

In 1861 old shotguns, squirrel rifles, smoothbores from the Mexican War, and even flintlocks from Revolutionary days, perched atop the shoulders of the drilling volunteers. Most soldiers regarded this hodge-podge with universal contempt. "Miserable old thing," one Yank called his imported Belgian musket. He said that it would "do about as much execution to the shooter as the shootee." Another private called his first weapon "the poorest excuse of a gun I ever saw." Some of these early pieces were as small as .32 caliber, while others stretched up to a massive .75. "Infinitely more dangerous to friend than enemy," one observer said of them, and General U.S. Grant disapprovingly remarked that a man might "fire at you all day without you ever finding it out." No wonder the soldiers called such weapons "mules" and "pumpkin slingers." Belgian and Austrian rifles, largely in .54 caliber, were far too heavy, clumsy, badly made and inaccurate. Soldiers called them "European stovepipes," and happily discarded them when Springfields and Enfields became available. Other British imports fared better, like the Whitworth and Brunswick rifles and the Kerr. Meanwhile,

LEFT: Looking the properly-outfitted and gallant soldier, this New York militiaman bears his 1861 model Springfield proudly, complete with glistening bayonet. By war's end he would discard much of this, but treat his gun like a brother.

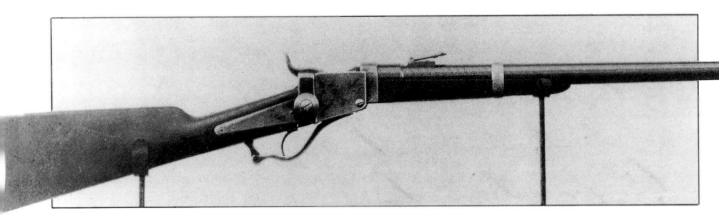

LEFT: A host of experimental shoulder arms were introduced during the war, and many, such as this Starr carbine prototype, were subjected to War Department tests. It would pass, and go on to see limited use with mounted forces.

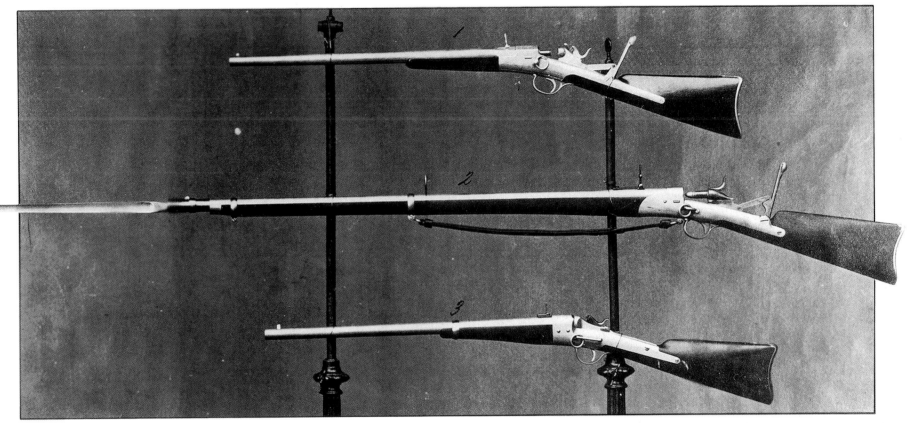

American inventors North and South strove to fill the need with new designs of their own, and produced a dazzling variety of models. Most of the new designs were attempts at breechloaders, using the newly-developed, self-contained cartridge, usually a powder charge contained in a brass or copper casing, with a percussion cap built into the base, and a lead bullet extending from the opposite end. There was the Greene rifle, the Burnside, and most especially the Sharps, the latter used to arm a number of Union regiments, and spawning a Confederate copy.

In the South, manufacturers were severely limited by failing machinery and scarcity of raw materials. Consequently, most stuck with the simpler muzzle-loading design. Variations were produced, almost always in small numbers, by the Richmond Armory, the Fayetteville, North Carolina, Arsenal, the Georgia Armory, and by firms like Read and Watson, Cook and Brothers, H.C. Lamb, Morse,

ABOVE: Some inventors submitted a variety of models to government inspectors. Allen's rifle patent was added to Brand's breech-loader to make a .44 carbine (top), a .54 rifle (center), and a .54 carbine (bottom). In the end, none were adopted, in common with most of this inventor's dreams.

Chapman, and more. Some produced no more than a few dozen before their machinery failed, or Union invaders put them out of business.

Both sides also armed cavalrymen, and occasionally artillerymen, with shoulder arms, usually simple, shortened versions of the long arms, and called either carbines or musketoons. The reduced length, sometimes to barely more than half that of the infantry weapon, made them more manageable by men on horses, and lighter in weight. Having abandoned his saber, the cavalryman placed his greatest reliance on his carbine, which he usually fired not from horseback, but from the

ground. The Sharps carbine was a favorite among Yankee horsemen, most of whom had breechloaders of one pattern or another, including the Starr, the Maynard, the Gallager, the Joslyn, and the Burnside, all of them with shortened wooden stocks to further lighten their weight, and generally in calibers like .54 or less.

It was also in the Union cavalry that the most ambitious of the war's innovations took a firm hold. The concept of repeating rifles, adding rate of fire to the new accuracy, was not exactly new, but practical systems that would operate dependably without fouling and jamming proved very elusive, making

ABOVE: This fanciful print depicting Union cavalrymen firing from the saddle with their carbines runs counter to the fact that cavalrymen generally fought dismounted, like the horseman on the facing page, in a battlefield park sculpture. The horse provided mobility, the carbine lightweight firepower, but to be effective it had to be fired from an immobile position.

RIGHT: At the close of the war, an endless line of stands of Union Springfields act as silent sentinel outside the Petersburg, Va., railroad depot. For all of the variety of firearms used, it was this weapon that carried the brunt of the Federal war effort. With the war done, hundreds of thousands of them were turned to more peaceful purposes. FACING PAGE: The Confederate trenches at Petersburg yielded up the dead who fell in the last days before the collapse of April 1865. Beside them lay their rifles, primarily Enfields like these, most of them destined for destruction, or decay in warehouses. Already, developments in weapons technology was making Springfield, Enfield and all of their kind obsolete.

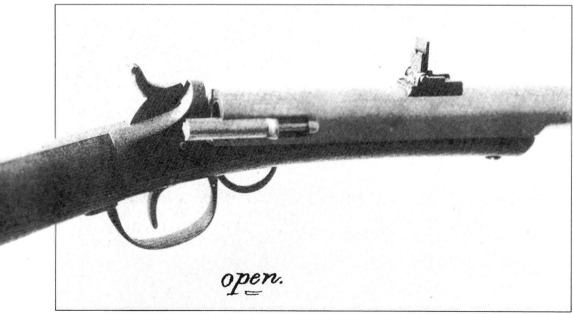

open.

ABOVE: Lee's breech-loading carbine, another invention that never caught on, but the war had spurred the inventors' minds, and now they could not be stopped.

army officials wary of taking a risk. But a cavalryman needed rate of fire to improve the effectiveness of his mounted mobility, and thus it was that the Union War Department decided to experiment with the new Spencer repeating rifle. It was an unqualified success. Samuel Colt had already adapted his revolver principle to make five-shot repeating rifles, but they were prone to burn the shooter when fired. Spencer's system was much more efficient, and safer. A tubular magazine was inserted through the butt of the stock, and then the simple operation of a lever, doubling as a trigger guard, expelled the spent cartridge and loaded the new one. The hammer had to be cocked after each firing, but still a man could pour out seven shots almost as fast as he could jerk the lever.

The cavalrymen loved the Spencer, as did the few infantry regiments armed with a longer rifle version. "The Rebs made three charges on us but we stood up to the rack with our 7 Shooters & repulsed them each time," wrote one Billy Yank. "The Rebs hate our guns they call them the Yankee 7 Devils." Well over 100,000 of them saw service in the Union Army, and with devastating effect.

Even greater firepower came from the new Henry rifle. It was a heavy gun, being almost all iron and brass and weighing 9.8 pounds. But part of that weight was also a hefty fifteen rounds of .44 ammunition that a soldier could fire off even faster

than with a Spencer. A lever below the trigger simply moved forward and back, cocking the rifle, ejecting a spent shell, and inserting a new one. One quick motion, and the rifle was ready to fire again. One practiced soldier was clocked at loading and firing 120 rounds in five minutes, 45 seconds, a rate better than one shot every three seconds! The Henry could jam easily, and the Union war

FACING PAGE: Soldiers returning home took with them memories of innumerable scenes like this one of Federal drilling outside Washington. For four years their rifles had been their closest companions, and often their most trustworthy friends. Indeed, men who could, often took their rifles home with them.

department did not trust either its reliability or the bill for all the ammunition it could consume. Barely more than 10,000 were issued to Northern soldiers, most purchased by individual states like Illinois. A few years after the war, with the Winchester Model 1873, it would go on to become the rifle that won the West. Ironically, while military men continued to distrust weapons offering speed and volume of fire in long arms, they had accepted the favorability of such things in handguns for more than a decade.

ABOVE: The capture of Confederate Lieutenant H. J. Segal. No tree was high enough to escape the threat of a couple of Springfields aimed at a man, whatever his rank, and their accuracy changed the nature of warfare in America irrevocably.

CHAPTER TWENTY TWO

HANDGUNS

ABOVE: Uriah Crawford of Company K, 54th Virginia Infantry was not, as an infantryman, authorized by regulations to carry a handgun.

Up until the Mexican War in 1846-48, military handguns had been almost exclusively single shot – first flintlock, and then percussion – often using the same lock and the same caliber as the rifles made at United States armories. Attempts at inventing practical repeaters, or multi-shot pistols, came forth intermittently, but it was not until the 1830s, with the development of the percussion system, that Samuel Colt patented the first practical revolver, the so-called Patterson. He soon improved upon it dramatically, and by 1848 had patented his .44 caliber 3d Model Army revolver, sometimes called a dragoon pistol thanks to its being issued to United

States Dragoon regiments before the Civil War. With a host of variations and refinements, it would dominate revolver design and function down to the present.

As with shoulder arms at the outset of the war, 1861, saw a host of ersatz handguns go to war with the first volunteers. A few carried old flintlock Harpers Ferry pistols dating back nearly to the turn of the century. More carried single-shot percussion pieces, especially military weapons like the Springfield Model 1855, .58 caliber pistol-carbine, nothing more than a standard Springfield lock and short barrel, on a wooden pistol stock, with a detachable shoulder stock that would allow the

piece to be aimed and fired almost like a rifle.

But few cavalry units were privately raised or equipped in the Civil War, and since the two governments raised most mounted units, they equipped them with revolvers. By an overwhelming majority, the various patterns of Colt pistols dominated sidearms on both sides. More than 150,000 of them saw service, both as cavalrymen's handguns, and as officers' sidearms. They came in bore sizes from .36 to .44, chiefly in the Model 1851 in the former caliber, also called the "Navy," and in the Model 1860 .44 "Army."

The Colts were simplicity itself. They were "single-action," meaning that drawing back the hammer turned the cylinder from one chamber to the next after firing. Pulling the trigger was a separate action. A few "double-action" revolvers, wherein pulling hard on the trigger did everything, were used, but they did not gain favor. Almost all Colts were six-shooters, though a few with five chambers were made. A nipple sat at the back of each chamber, requiring a percussion cap. A ramming lever under the barrel pressed home each load, most often a paper "cartridge" containing ball and powder charge.

ABOVE: The age-old rivalry of infantry and cavalry was mocked good-naturedly by these two Yankees, with the horse soldier getting the upper hand with his Model 1852 Colt Navy .36. A man almost needed such point-blank range to ensure a hit, for the short barrel and unsteadiness of the arm worked against accuracy at a distance.

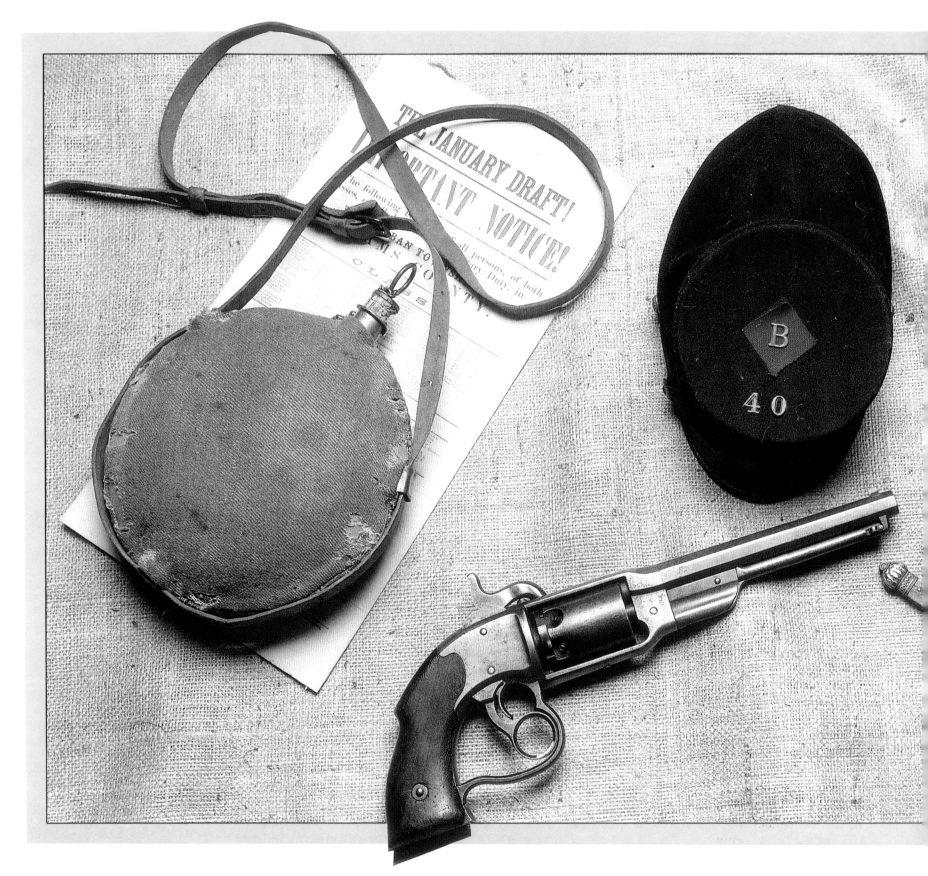

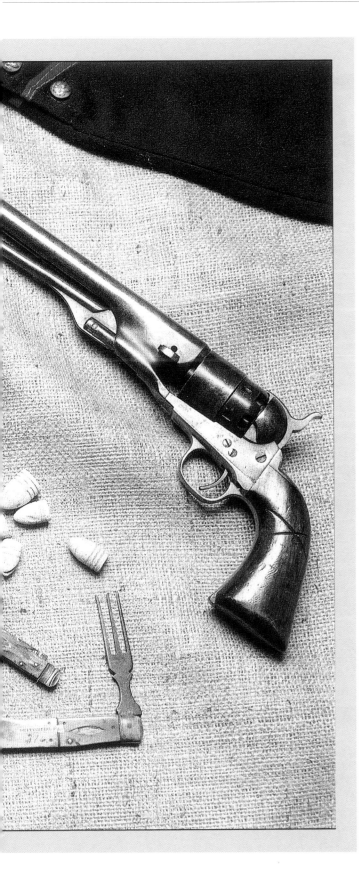

The pistol could be fired as fast as one could cock the hammer and pull the trigger. Then, of course, it was a somewhat time-consuming process to reload the cylinder, and black powder being a messy business at best when fired, a build-up of grimy fouling could slow or even stop a revolver's functioning until thoroughly cleaned. Consequently, many troopers carried fully-loaded spare cylinders with them. After firing all the loads in one, it was a simple and quick process to remove the bolt holding the barrel to the frame, slide off the empty cylinder, slide a new one on, and replace the barrel. It could be done in thirty seconds, and the revolver was ready for action again.

The Colt in its several forms predominated in both Union and Confederate armies. Indeed, early in 1861 Colt and other Northern arms manufacturers actually filled orders for pistols from Southern state militia leaders, and thereafter many more were taken from captured or fallen Billy Yanks, making a Northern handgun the weapon of choice among Rebel troopers and officers.

If Colt dominated the field, still he did not monopolize it. A major competitor for army contracts in the North was the Remington firm, whose revolver was very similar in many respects, but slightly sturdier from the fact that the barrel was permanently fixed. Far fewer Remingtons found their way into Southern hands, but they were prized when they did.

Unable to purchase Colt revolvers after 1861, a number of Southern manufacturers attempted to make their own, some with considerable success. Griswold and Gunnison of Griswoldville, Georgia, made an excellent copy of the Colt Navy in a .44 model, substituting brass for the iron frame. Rigdon and Ansley, and later Leech and Rigdon, made a similar copy with iron frame. J.H. Dance & Brothers made both .36 and .44 caliber copies. The Columbus, Georgia, Firearms Manufacturing Company, Tucker, Sherrard & Company, Clark, Sherrard & Company, and several others also followed suit, some even copying the earlier 1848 dragoon models. Meanwhile, T.W. Cofer and the Spiller and Burr firm made versions based on the Remington. All of these and more were produced in very limited numbers, again thanks to scarcity of raw materials and

LEFT: Pistols, like their shoulder arm counterparts and edged weapons, appeared on the battlefields and in the camps in a dazzling variety. The Colt New Model Army 1860 pistol (at right), in .44 caliber, was the most commonly seen sidearm in the Union military among officers, and even in some cavalry units. By contrast, the distinctive Savage revolver (at left) was carried by only a few, and mostly as a privately purchased arm. The middle finger drew back the ring below the trigger, turning the cylinder, and then the index finger fired the gun. It should have been effective, but it was not, and it lagged far behind the Colt models in popularity.

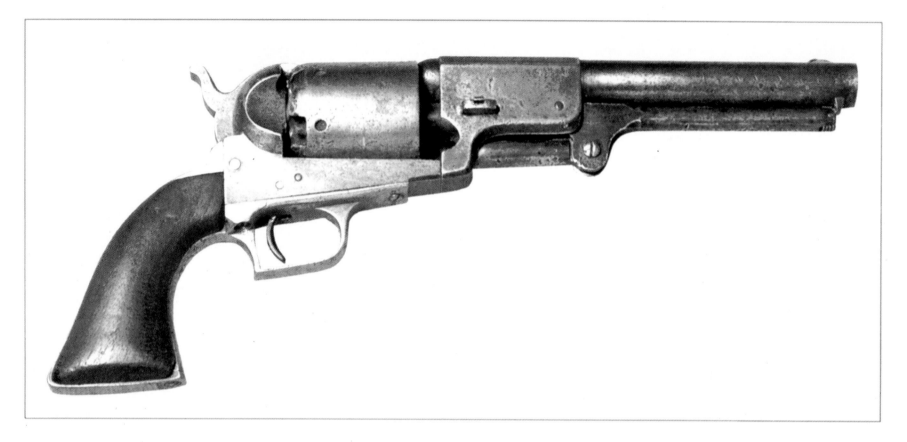

ABOVE: This Colt 2d Model Dragoon pistol, caliber .44, was one of a series, starting with the 1846 Colt Walker, that showed a steady progression and refinement of pistol design by Colt as he made his pistols lighter and easier to manage, without reducing firepower substantially. This was still a weighty handgun, but effective enough for the Confederates to copy it with their Tucker, Sherrard model.

machinery. Moreover, when the weapons broke down, spare parts were even more scarce. To help fill the gap between production and demand, several Confederate arms makers also produced limited numbers of older, single shot patterns.

Firms like Smith and Wesson, Starr, and others, also provided pistols to the Union service, some of them quite exotic, like the Savage, which had two finger levers, one for rotating the cylinder and cocking the piece, and the other for firing. Somewhat similar in appearance was the Butterfield Army Revolver, while other makers like Plant and Sharps, and the Manhattan Arms Company, came forward with their own designs. Among the most unusual were the pistols with knife blades that folded back alongside the barrel, providing an edged weapon once the pistol was discharged. And even the older "pepperbox" pistol, with six or more barrels comprising the revolving cylinder, saw some use.

North and South also looked to foreign makers to provide them with cavalry pistols. British pistols were especially popular. The Kerr .44 revolver saw some use, and even more of the Webley .44s, one of

the few double-actions used, were imported. The Beaumont-Adams also came into play, and several versions of the popular Tranter revolver went into action. This last came in a single-trigger model, single-action, and a so-called "double-trigger" version, on which the middle finger pulled a lower trigger, cocking the hammer and turning the cylinder, and then the index finger pulled a firing trigger.

The French, too, provided pistols, mostly ineffective and unpopular Lefaucheaux "pin-fire" models that used a forty-year-old system involving a self-contained brass cartridge with a small pin protruding from the side at the base. This acted as a percussion cap when struck by the hammer. Far more popular among French creations, and one of the most storied handguns of the entire war, was the LeMat. It was the invention of a French military man who tried to provide the maximum of firepower in a handgun. The cylinder itself carried up to nine .40 caliber loads. That, in itself, was intimidating. But LeMat did not stop there. Under the barrel he placed a tube for an .18 gauge shotgun load. When

LEFT: Two Confederate cavalrymen, probably from a Mississippi outfit, sit calmly for the camera with their pistols in their belts. The man on the right appears to have a Colt Model 1851 Navy revolver, caliber .36, though it may be a .44-caliber version. His friend on the left is carrying a smaller version, probably the Colt Model 1849 Pocket revolver. Though the Confederates had a number of private manufacturers who made copies of the Colt patterns, output was always small and quality generally inferior. Furthermore, while the original Colts in these models had octagonal barrels, almost all Confederate copies had round barrels.

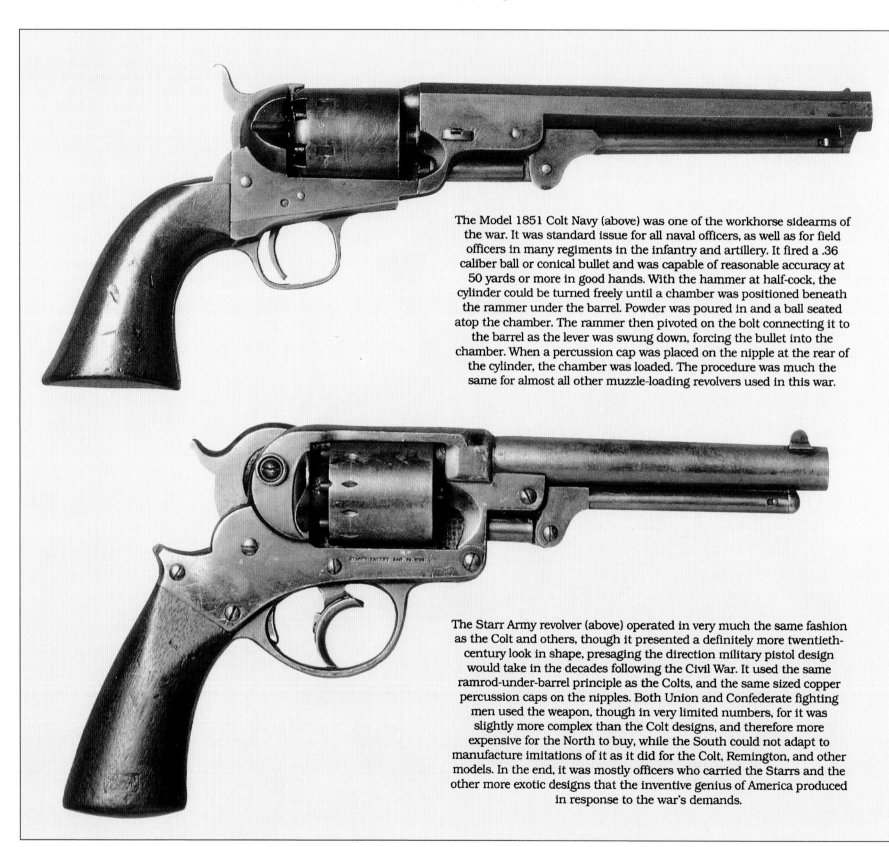

The Model 1851 Colt Navy (above) was one of the workhorse sidearms of the war. It was standard issue for all naval officers, as well as for field officers in many regiments in the infantry and artillery. It fired a .36 caliber ball or conical bullet and was capable of reasonable accuracy at 50 yards or more in good hands. With the hammer at half-cock, the cylinder could be turned freely until a chamber was positioned beneath the rammer under the barrel. Powder was poured in and a ball seated atop the chamber. The rammer then pivoted on the bolt connecting it to the barrel as the lever was swung down, forcing the bullet into the chamber. When a percussion cap was placed on the nipple at the rear of the cylinder, the chamber was loaded. The procedure was much the same for almost all other muzzle-loading revolvers used in this war.

The Starr Army revolver (above) operated in very much the same fashion as the Colt and others, though it presented a definitely more twentieth-century look in shape, presaging the direction military pistol design would take in the decades following the Civil War. It used the same ramrod-under-barrel principle as the Colts, and the same sized copper percussion caps on the nipples. Both Union and Confederate fighting men used the weapon, though in very limited numbers, for it was slightly more complex than the Colt designs, and therefore more expensive for the North to buy, while the South could not adapt to manufacture imitations of it as it did for the Colt, Remington, and other models. In the end, it was mostly officers who carried the Starrs and the other more exotic designs that the inventive genius of America produced in response to the war's demands.

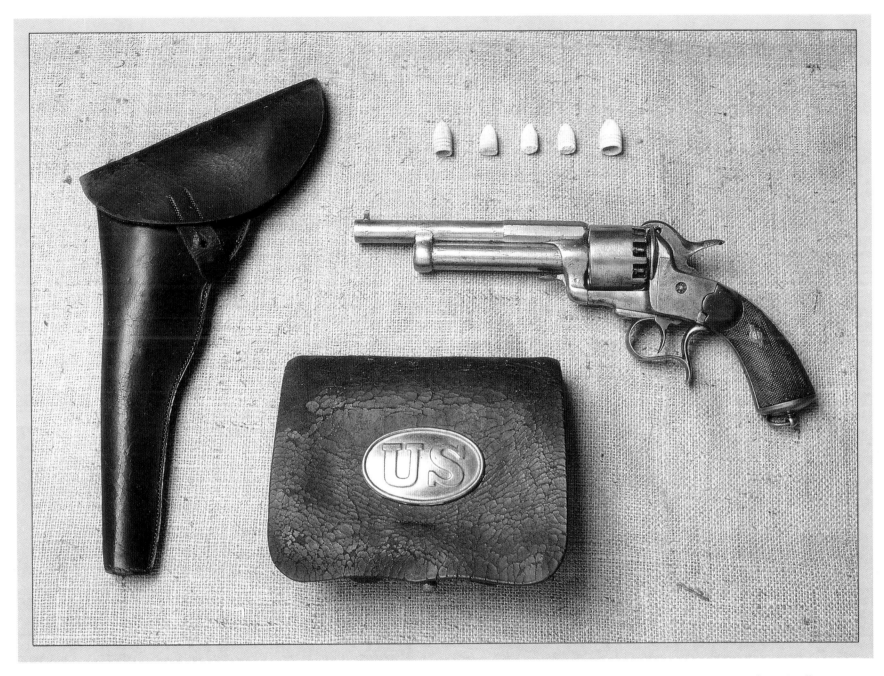

the shooter had exhausted the chambers in the cylinder, he had simply to cock the hammer again, bend down an extension hinged to its nose, and pull the trigger. The extension would strike a stationary nipple at the base of the cylinder pin ... and a deadly scatter load was launched toward the foe.

LeMat had tried to market a rifle and carbine version of his invention, but it was terribly heavy, with not one, but two full-length steel barrels. And the system was cumbersome to load. Even the pistol never saw more than limited use, being expensive, and the .40 bore size more difficult to provide ammunition for. Most were purchased privately by officers. General P.G.T. Beauregard carried one, though he never fired it in anger. However, Major General James Ewell Brown "Jeb" Stuart, Lee's fighting cavalry commander, carried and used a LeMat until his death.

ABOVE: One of the deadliest handguns of the war was the French-made LeMat revolver. Immediately beneath the main barrel sat an 18 gauge shotgun barrel on which the cylinder revolved. When the nine loads in the cylinder were exhausted, an adjustment of the hammer brought the scatter load to bear.

CHAPTER TWENTY-THREE

ARTILLERY

Even the ambitious Colonel LeMat could not create a handgun that would match the firepower of the really big guns: the cannon. If one of the holdovers from Napoleonic tactics was the notion of the bayonet deciding battles, another was that artillery was second only to thunderbolts in effectiveness.

The truth of the matter was otherwise. By the time of the Civil War, technology had advanced the big guns very little since the time of Napoleon. While a wonderful variety of designs was available, all but a few operated on the same principle of the first artillery pieces centuries before. A hollow tube, either of brass, bronze, or iron, was open at one end

TOP: A row of light 12-pounders and caissons in 1864. **ABOVE**: The Washington Arsenal in 1864. **FACING PAGE**: A Union field battery ready for action.

and closed at the other. A bag of black powder was rammed into the muzzle, the open end, and shoved to the back of the tube. The projectile was pushed in after it. Most of the tubes were smooth bores; a few had rifling. The piece was simply detonated either by the old-fashioned method of applying a flame or lit fuze to a touch-hole at the breech, or, more often, a copper priming fuze was inserted into the vent, and its spark set off by jerking a friction primer. The result was a deafening roar, a cloud of thick, white smoke that hung low over the battlefield, and a jet of flame thirty yards long as the projectile rushed forth on its mission. The projectiles, too, differed little from

RIGHT: A hint of the sight and sound of a cannon discharging, as a gun crew fires a light field piece. Bits of wadding and paper fly out the barrel, along with an acrid plume of smoke. Hundreds of such guns could turn a battlefield into a nightmarish cloud.

those of earlier generations, being only sometimes larger and a bit more reliable. There was the solid shot, literally a round ball of iron, and of little effect except when it hit an opposing artillery piece – and of course, any unfortunate man in its path. Other loads were designed to be more effective as anti-personnel weapons. The shell, either round or, occasionally, cylindroconoidal, was hollow inside and contained a powder charge. A timed fuze in its

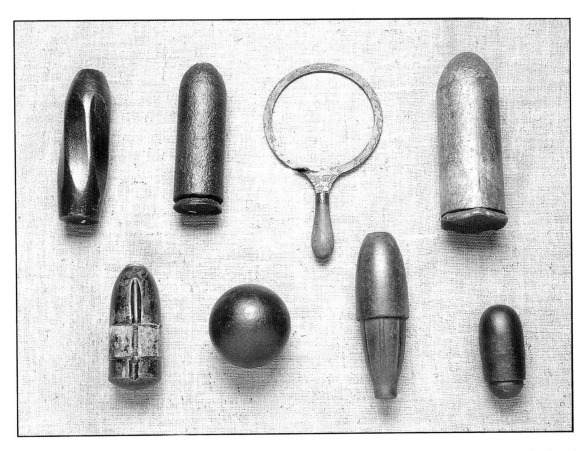

ABOVE: Just some of the cannoneer's wares. At top left is a shell for a Whitworth rifle. Beside it are two Parrott shells and a round gauge for measuring shot sizes. Beneath at left is a 3-inch rifle bolt, then a solid shot, a Schenkl shell, and probably a Britten shell from England.

base was theoretically ignited at firing, and when the interior charge went off, the shell flew apart into a dozen or more pieces. Unfortunately, fuzes were notoriously unreliable, sometimes no more than one in fifteen actually working. On top of that, the estimates of timing by gunners could be off, the trajectory of the gun faulty, and the shell might bury itself in the ground before going off, if it exploded at all, thus doing little or no harm.

More effective was spherical case shot, again a round ball, but this time hollow and containing up to 78 lead musket balls and an exploding charge.

When it went off in the midst of a line of soldiers, this could be deadly, though many of the balls flew straight up into the air and others straight down into the ground, doing nothing, while of the rest, only those at the forward and sides of the moving ball had any chance of killing or injuring. Of the 78 bullets, probably no more than a third had even the potential of putting men out of action. Grapeshot, large iron balls two inches in diameter and arranged in "stands" of a dozen or more, was not much used in the Civil War, but a cousin called canister was the most damaging of all artillery loads. On top of the powder charge in a smoothbore, the gunners would ram down a tin can filled with 27 cast iron balls, each nearly half a pound in weight. The load was used against attacking infantry when within 300 yards or less. On being fired, it turned the cannon into a huge shotgun.

FACING PAGE: A battery of Wiard guns at the Washington Arsenal, one of many experimental designs tried by the Union artillery. ABOVE: 20-pounder Parrott rifles of the 1st New York Artillery. The reinforcing band around the breech is clearly evident, adding strength to the design and allowing the massive loads to drive the rifle's projectiles great distances with accuracy. LEFT: Battery A of the 4th United States Artillery near Brandy Station, Virginia, in September 1863, with an older model 12-pounder howitzer.

MAIN PICTURE: A Yankee artillery battery preparing to go into action on June 4, 1863, on the south bank of the Rappahannock River, unaware that the Confederates were then moving north toward Gettysburg. These 12-pounder "Napoleons" show how much space a battery in action required, not only for the guns, but also for the ammunition chests and caissons to the rear, not to mention the animals.

INSET LEFT: A stately row of Parrott rifles, ordnance rifles, and other types, in a Civil War battlefield park. **INSET CENTER:** Twelve-pounders in the Confederate defense works ringing Atlanta in 1864. Most cannon in such positions saw little action, for officers were reluctant to storm such works. **INSET RIGHT:** A Yankee battery standing in defense on Malvern Hill in 1862, giving Lee his first defeat of the war.

BOTTOM: A massive 8-inch Brooke rifle prepared for transport on a Confederate gun sling, as they appeared when captured on the James River. As such carts testified, there was no escaping the massive weights faced by artillerymen. **BELOW**: It took at least two men, and a special grip, just to carry some of the projectiles fired by these monster guns.

The artillery of both sides in the war was dominated by a basic fieldpiece design little changed from the time of Napoleon and, in fact, named for him. The Model 1841 gun-howitzer in several variants, most especially the Model 1857 12-pounder Napoleon, was the workhorse of Union and Confederate artillery. It combined the longer range of the old standard gun with the lighter weight and somewhat higher trajectory of the howitzer. It took its nickname from the great exponent of artillery, and the 12-pounder reference derived from the 12.3 pound solid shot that it fired. It had a smooth bore of 4.62 inches, weighed 1,227 pounds exclusive of its two-wheeled wooden carriage, and twice a minute could fire a projectile out of its bronze tube, sending it up to 1,600 yards. It was simplicity itself, and indestructible. Its carriage generally wore out long before the gun tube. The Union manufactured over 1,100 Napoleons, at a cost of about $600 apiece. The Confederate foundries made another 500 or more, using everything from bronze, to brass, to cast iron.

Such smoothbore fieldpieces also came in smaller, 6-pounder, variants, and all the way up to 24- and even 32-pounder howitzer sizes. All were used essentially the same way and for the same

ABOVE: Massive animal power was needed to transport some of these giants, like the Rodman smoothbore seacoast columbiad being pulled through a Washington street in this photograph. Such guns were big enough for a man to climb inside, but rarely saw action as they were reserved for guarding fortifications, chiefly in the North. **LEFT**: Much more lively careers awaited naval guns like this Dahlgren "soda pop bottle" gun aboard the Yankee gunboat *Hunchback* on the James River. The gigantic screw mechanism at the breech is for raising and lowering the piece to aim it. Only by using levers and screws could mortal men wield these many-ton weapons.

purposes. Much larger smoothbores, monsters with bores up to 20 inches and more in diameter, and capable of firing projectiles weighing more than half a ton, were built for seacoast defense in the North and to protect large stationary fortifications. One Isaac Rodman smoothbore was capable of hurling a ball nearly five miles out to sea – farther than anyone could see for aiming! These massive columbiads, as they were sometimes called, rarely fired in anger.

More often used were their short, stubby cousins, the mortars. Fat and squat, these weapons had a very specific purpose. They were designed to sit low to the ground, and to fire a heavy exploding ball high up into the air in an arching trajectory that could take it over and behind earthworks or masonry fortifications, to explode in their rear. Very few traveled with field armies, for they were of no use in

FACING PAGE: A brace of 3-inch ordnance rifles peer across the fields of a Civil War battlefield, much as they did in the 1860s. By contrast, the mammoth 13-inch mortar above is truly awesome. It weighed 17,000 pounds, could only be transported by rail, and was used almost exclusively for battering fortifications. LEFT: A Rodman smoothbore seacoast columbiad on its iron carriage in the Washington defenses. Such weapons could fire projectiles further than the eye could see.

ARTILLERY

BELOW: A huge, 15-inch Rodman being tested at Fort Monroe, Virginia. The block and tackle needed to hoist the projectile to the muzzle testifies to the weight of its shot. Such guns, however, were almost exclusively fired for practice, never coming under attack from either land or sea. RIGHT: Outside Washington a fort displays a stand of the massive shells for the big guns, each equipped with special gripping holes for the tongs needed to hoist it. FAR RIGHT: Early in the war seacoast cannon looked more like this early model, whose shot could be handled by a single man.

conventional battles. But when it came time for a siege, as at Vicksburg and Petersburg, then the mortar came into its own, and they, too, came in sizes up to 13 inches, some even being mounted on flatboats or railroad flat cars for greater speed and mobility.

Newer technological innovations vied for the attentions of the artillerists. The rifling revolution was not restricted just to shoulder arms. Many experimental models had been tested prior to the war, but when the conflict came, inventors and manufacturers rushed to get into production. Quickly the 3-inch ordnance rifle came to be the favored piece. Its 3-inch bore, with deep rifling grooves, imparted a spin to its elongated shells that gave them greatly increased range and accuracy. It

FACING PAGE: An artist's conception of part of the battlefield at Fredericksburg, Virginia, in December 1862, when Confederate artillery probably did more damage to the Union army than in any other fight of the war. Placed on heights and well served, field pieces could be deadly. **ABOVE:** The Union 13-inch mortar "Dictator," in operation during the siege of Petersburg. It was the most photographed cannon of the war. **LEFT:** Yankee mortars waiting to be moved and mounted near Dutch Gap, Virginia, in 1864.

RIGHT: Battery B, 1st Pennsylvania Light Artillery, either in action or awaiting action on the front at Petersburg in 1864. Though clearly a "posed" photograph, it nevertheless shows the gunners in their positions, and some of their 12-pounder field pieces. Interestingly, the famed photographer Mathew Brady is in the scene, seventh from the right, immediately behind the center cannon. Moments after the scene was taken, Confederates supposedly opened fire.

BELOW: Just as with small arms, the Civil War produced a host of experimental cannon, most of them tending toward the breech-loader in design. One such was Lee's Breechloader, whose mechanism allowed the massive block at the rear to tip downward for inserting a shot or shell. Like the majority of designs, it was rejected and never went into production.

was lighter in weight than a Napoleon, and used a smaller charge, its wrought iron tube fitting the contours of the rifled projectile so closely that maximum efficiency was derived from the powder charge.

Equally as popular was the ten-pounder Parrott rifle, named for its inventor Robert Parrott. It was a cast iron tube, with a wrought iron band around the breech, reinforcing it for large loads. This allowed it to use the same projectile and the same load as the ordnance rifle, while gaining nearly 100 extra yards in range, up to 1,900. The Parrotts were made in a number of sizes all the way up to massive 300-pounders. While the Confederates tried to copy the Parrott, they did not have sufficient facilities or machinery to do so in numbers. Indeed, for their rifled cannon the Rebels depended heavily upon British imports, especially Blakely and Armstrong guns, most of which used variations of the Parrott reinforcing principal.

TOP LEFT: Mann's Breechloader was another experimental design that was never adopted. A crank loosened the breech block, which pivoted downward to expose the tube for loading. Mann's design was submitted in June 1865, when interest was dwindling with the end of the war. **TOP RIGHT**: The Broadwell Breechloader fared no better, though it was a simpler design. A slide pulled aside in a slot in the breech to open up the tube. After the charge was inserted, the slide was pushed back in and the gun fired. It would have allowed one of the fastest rates of fire of any cannon of the war if successful and adopted. **LEFT**: It remained for the conventional old designs to bear the brunt of duty in the Civil War, on both sides. Giants like this 100-pounder Parrott rifle at Fort Brady, Virginia, represented less a state-of-the-art than a state-of-acceptance, but they were enough to do the job.

MAIN PICTURE: Redan Number 11 in the siege works surrounding Petersburg, Virginia. Photographer Mathew Brady, wearing the straw hat, stands at center, with a battery of 12-pounders behind him ready for action, though not at the moment under fire, as attested by the men casually lounging atop the earthworks.

INSET LEFT: The burst breech of an experimental cannon made of steel and cast iron combined. Metallurgy was not yet up to the strains that newly-refined powders could produce. **INSET RIGHT**: An earthwork protecting a battery emplacement, as reconstructed on a Civil War park site. Gunners guarded their pieces jealously.

ABOVE: A British Armstrong gun at Fort Fisher, North Carolina, an example of the banded reinforced rifles put into use by the Confederates.

FACING PAGE: Richmond at the end of the war, with the ruins of some of its arsenal, and munitions in the foreground.

The Armstrong also illustrated another innovation, the breechloader. Hoping to allow for greater rate of fire, Armstrong designed a powerful hollow screw for the breech of his gun. When cranked back, it allowed a solid breechblock to be removed, the projectile and charge shoved in, and the breechblock replaced. Cranking the screw back tightly, the piece was ready to fire. Even more innovative was the Whitworth, whose threaded breechblock unscrewed and turned to the side for loading. Unfortunately the breechloaders proved to be temperamental and only a few were ever used. Lee did have two with the Army of Northern Virginia, each capable of firing up to six miles – not much of an advantage when a battlefield gunner could rarely see more than half a mile in any direction.

CHAPTER TWENTY–FOUR

"INFERNAL MACHINES"

The inventors who turned their imaginations to weapons went considerably beyond conventional innovation in the hope of winning military contracts. To artillerists, especially, they looked for inspiration. Many tried new kinds of exploding shells, some with incendiary charges like the ancient "Greek fire," designed to set ablaze fortifications. Others tried joining two solid shot with a length of chain, expecting that upon firing the balls would stretch the chain, start spinning, and thus mow their way through infantry. At least one double-barreled fieldpiece was tried, expected to fire each tube simultaneously and send solid shot, linked by chain, through the foe. All such

TOP: The Adams hand grenade, and the leather strap that ignited its fuze when thrown. **ABOVE:** The interior of the Adams grenade, a cannonball filled with shot.

efforts failed, one observer noting that when the double-barreled cannon was test fired, it plowed up a field, knocked over a couple of saplings, and the the balls broke apart, one killing a nearby cow "while the other knocked down the chimney from a log cabin."

So did the attempts to make repeating cannon fail. Most tried the revolver principle, which meant welding several cannon barrels together, an awkward and incredibly cumbersome concept. H.C. Pate of Petersburg, Virginia, did design a cannon with a crank operated revolving cylinder at its rear, but only two were made, and when the first exploded, killing half its crew, the other was

retired as a curiosity.

Nevertheless, the idea of a stationary, mounted repeater remained persistent, and if it could not be applied practically to large bores for cannon projectiles, still inventors found ways of making what were, in effect, the precursors of machine guns. Some were so simple as to be almost crude. The Billinghurst Requa Battery was perhaps the simplest of all. It consisted of little more than 25 .58 caliber rifle barrels mounted parallel to one another on a horizontal bed. A "clip" holding 25 steel-bound cartridges was fitted into a sliding breech, and

when a lever was pulled, the bullets slid into their barrels. Then came the problem. The gunner had to pour a train of powder behind the breech and ignite it with a percussion cap. Rain, wind and carelessness could all prevent the powder from igniting, or all barrels from going off at once. Supposedly the Requa was capable of seven volleys a minute, but the few put into action, mostly in South Carolina by Federal troops, achieved far less. Seeing little real action, it was often posted in defense of narrow openings and confined spaces like bridges, leading to its sobriquet of the "covered bridge gun."

ABOVE: One of the war's most interesting attempts at increased firepower was the Requa Battery, really just a lot of rifle barrels on a carriage, with a special means of loading and firing. The cartridges were loaded into the frames shown on the ground, then inserted with one movement, and fired by another, as the frame of spent casings on the right testifies.

ABOVE: The "Steam gun," invented by Marylander Ross Winans, would use steam pressure rather than gunpowder to propel its shot, but it never saw service and was impractical in any case.
RIGHT: The so-called "Wire gun" was also a failure, as this burst prototype shows. It sought to reinforce the barrel for heavy charges by using tightly-wrapped steel wire.

The Vandenburg Volley Gun was even less effective. It had anywhere from 85 to a staggering 451 barrels clustered, row upon row, in a cylindrical container. When the breechblock was opened, a container with all the charges was inserted, the block closed again, and a single percussion hammer set off the whole conglomeration. It was painfully slow to load, and only effective for rapid fire if several magazines were pre-loaded and ready for insertion. Worse, it had no "spread" in its firing pattern. It was accurate enough, and at 100 yards could group more than ninety percent of its bullets in a six foot square. In battle, of course, that meant that only one or two men would actually be hit, though any man inside that six-foot square did not have much of a life expectancy.

The Confederates experimented with a rapid-fire, large-bore cannon called the Williams Machine Gun, which theoretically could fire more than sixty 1.57 caliber balls per minute. A gunner operated the crank that opened the breech block, and cocked a hammer, while another man inserted the paper-wrapped cartridge and capped a nipple. Closing the crank closed the block and tripped the hammer. Few were used, and they proved to be temperamental. Much more efficient was the Agar Machine Gun, which looked for all the world like a crank operated coffee mill. It could shoot 120 .58 bullets per minute, the turning of a crank feeding each cartridge down from a hopper into the chamber, and then firing it. As the crank continued turning, the spent casing was ejected and the next cartridge inserted.

The most practical design of all came along too late for wide use in the war, and it is just as well for the men who would have had to face it. The Gatling Gun was first patented in 1862. It had six barrels mounted to make a hollow cylinder. Turning a crank rotated the barrels, and as each one came in line, the crank fed a cartridge from a hopper into the breech of the barrel and fired it. When working properly it could fire its .58 loads as fast as a man could turn the crank. The government failed to adopt it, but a few were briefly put in service at Petersburg in 1864, when General Benjamin F. Butler bought his own. Not until 1865, and a new model, were all the imperfections worked out, at which time the Gatling became a truly devastating

TOP: One of the most interesting experiments was the Vandenburg Volley Gun, with its scores, even hundreds, of barrels clustered together. Three appear here, the one on the right loaded and ready, the one in center with breech open for loading, and the one at left showing the muzzle end. **ABOVE**: Shells of varying designs were also tried out, like the Pevey shell shown in cutaway with its fuze, and an intact shell on the right. **LEFT**: In the center row of this 1864 photo appear the component parts of a new shell fuze being tried out by the Union. It appears completed on the top row, along with the tool for screwing it into the shell, while the bottom row shows it inserted into a variety of projectiles.

ABOVE: The artillery proving ground at Fort Monroe, Virginia, became a graveyard of inventors' hopes, littered with the ruins of one after another of the designs that failed. It was here that experiments were made with powder stress on accepted designs, seeing how much a gun could stand. The wreckage of a massive 15-inch Rodman remains after failing to stand up to an experimental charge. RIGHT: The Confederates experimented, too, but chiefly with deadly underwater devices like this "torpedo" found in the Potomac River and intended to sink Yankee shipping.

killing machine. Fortunately, the war was over by then.

Fortunately, too, a number of other dreadful innovations were still in their infancy. Hand grenades were tried, some with vanes and thrown like large darts, others nothing more than shells with lit fuzes. One invention called for a leather strap around a man's upper arm, its end attached to a friction primer in a shell. When he threw the shell, the strap yanked the primer as the shell left his hand, and a few seconds later – theoretically – the grenade went off. Other types called for a powder-filled sphere with 14 capped nipples protruding from it, to be enclosed in a larger, screw-capped, iron ball. Thrown – very gingerly, it must be said – it should go off when it hit the ground and one of the caps inevitably went off. The trouble was, it could just as easily go off when thrown or accidentally dropped.

As if all this were not enough, Confederate engineers also experimented with land mines, called

"torpedoes." On the Virginia Peninsula in the spring of 1862, General Gabriel J. Rians planted shells in the ground, with trip wires attached to fuzes. They were, arguably, the first "booby traps," and some were deadly effective. One Yankee officer wrote of seeing nothing but "a blood stain on the ground where a man was blown up." The use of such weapons was controversial, even in the Confederate high command, but then in a war in which technology was just as much a combatant as the armies themselves, almost anything could be deemed

legitimate. Even exploding bullets were attempted, designed to go off after entering a man's body.

No wonder, then, that more than 600,000 died. Though most were killed by disease, still a quarter million at least died as a result of wounds, almost one in ten of those who served. One in three could expect to be wounded at least once. Thus, no matter how ineffective or ill-used, how hare-brained or impractical many of the weapons of the American Civil War might have been, still they were more than equal to the task of maiming a generation.

ABOVE: Torpedoes were very simple, little more than wooden or iron barrels filled with gunpowder, and anchored to float just beneath the surface. They could be detonated electrically from the shore, or else by contact when a ship tripped a trigger and ignited a fuze.

CREDITS TO ILLUSTRATIONS

The publishers wish to thank the following individuals and organizations for granting permission to reproduce the illustrations in this book:

The Bettmann Archive; Bevoir-Jefferson Davis; Civil War Library and Museum, Philadelphia; *Civil War Times Illustrated*, Harrisburg, Pennsylvania; Chicago Historical Society; Confederate Hall and Museum; Confederate Memorial Hall, New Orleans; Delbert Crawford, 215 Gordon, Cary, N.C. 27511; Georgia Department of Archives and History; Collection of T. Gordon, Jr.; D. Mark Katz, Washington, D.C.; Kentucky Historical Library; John Henry Kurtz; Alvan Macauley, Grosse Point Farms, Michigan; Minnesota Historical Society; Missouri Historical Society; Museum of the Confederacy; National Archives, Washington, D.C.; National Library of Medicine, Bethesda, Maryland; The Naval Historical Center; New York Historical Society, New York City; Jon M. Nielson, Orono, Maine; Don Troiani; Tulane University, New Orleans; Bill Turner; U.S. Military Historical Institute, Carlisle, Pennsylvania; Valentine Musuem, Richmond, Virginia; Virginia Military Institute Museum; Virginia State Archives; Lee Wallace, 7626 Matera Street, Apt. 102, Falls Church, Virginia 22073; Western Reserve Historical Society, Cleveland, Ohio; Eugene Wooddell, Waukegan, Illinois; Wanda Wright, Phoenix, Arizona; Robert J. Younger, Dayton, Ohio.

ACKNOWLEDGMENTS

The publishers wish to thank the following for granting permission to photograph items from their collections: Chester County Historical Society, West Chester, Pennsylvania; The Civil War Library and Museum; J. Craig Nanos Collection; Virginia Historical Society; The Virginia Military Institute; New York State Division of Military and Naval Affairs; and the New York State Military Heritage Museum. Thanks are also due to the curatorial staff of West Point Museum, West Point, N.Y. for guidance and assistance in the preparation of uniform artworks, and to the Gettysburg National Park Service for their invaluable assistance.